# GYPSYGUISE & DISGUISE

**A HISTORY OF GYPSY FASHION**
by
**Juliet Jeffery**

Lamorna Publications

Lamorna Publications
Yew Tree Studio, Marshwood, Dorset DT6 5QF
www.lamornapublications.co.uk

First published in 2018
This edition 2021

ISBN: 978-0-9933898-5-6



Set in 11pt Times New Roman

# DEDICATION

1993

This book is dedicated to the memory of
Will and Rhona Taylor.

# CONTENTS

The vanity of dress in man is tickled not only by
his love of self-ornament but also by his desire
for social distinction.
DAR

# FOREWORD

## Damian le Bas

'Gypsy!' The word has been used to sell everything from high fashion collections to high street summer skirts, but the implication is always the same: buy this and you'll stand out.

This association of ethnic Gypsy life with unique styles of dress is centuries old. Laws passed during the reign of Henry VIII mention "outlandish people calling themselves Egyptians," and other evidence from the time suggests that Gypsies could be spotted a mile off because they didn't dress like anybody else. So, modern TV programmes that focus on brash Traveller styles aren't really saying anything new. The clothes themselves might change, but the desire not to look like the outsiders – the gaujos, gadje, buffers, non-Romany or country people – might have always been there, in one form or another.....as it still is.

Juliet Jeffery, on the other hand, has definitely done something new: producing a fully illustrated book that focuses on the history and evolution of Gypsy fashions. Make no mistake, this book is a one-off. It's a comprehensive look at Romany and Traveller dress down the centuries, up to the present day. It journeys from the earliest references to Gypsy attire in Mediaeval paintings and manuscripts, right up to the flash and brash 'race-day' outfits on show at twenty-first century horse fairs.

Lavishly illustrated with hundreds of the author's paintings, this book will be a revelation for those unfamiliar with Gypsy history, and full of surprises and new information for those who already know their stuff. It feels a bit ridiculous trying to do justice to this book with words alone. Like a sunny Saturday when Appleby Fair is in full swing, you really need to see it to believe it.

Her focus is on clothes, but by describing them in such depth, Juliet sheds light on other aspects of Gypsy culture. "The Gypsies brought from India three characteristics," she writes in the second chapter: "a conservatism or traditionalism, a love of jewellery and a partiality to bright colour." More specifically, they brought four particular items of clothing: "the women's scarf, the diklo (neckerchief) worn by men, the blanket for both sexes and the women's intricate plaited hairstyles and preference for long hair." As she also points out, it is the traditionalism – Gypsy people's tenacity in retaining old habits – that has kept so many of the other customs going. Much has changed down the centuries, with the result that today there is no such thing as simply "Gypsy dress;" and yet some of these items and tendencies have survived to a remarkable degree.

The book begins long ago, before the first large-scale arrival of Romany people in Britain (we should remember that at least one person of Romany heritage lived in East Anglia in the 11th century AD, and that non-Romany nomadic people were already living across these Isles long before that). There are various early 15th century references to dark-skinned bushy-bearded men arriving in various parts of continental Europe, and they attracted various names: Tartars, 'penancors,' strangers. Some wore two rings in each ear; others went about in "shifts tied on the shoulder with linen cords, and unusual short cloaks." A story of their being "Dukes of Lower Egypt" soon caught on. "Strange attire and garments" soon began to be seen as part and parcel of who the Gypsies were. This, combined with rumours that they had switched back and forth between Islam and Christianity in order to avoid persecution in different places, helped to generate an air of mystery and untrustworthiness.

Moving with a keen eye through rich historical evidence, Juliet refers to French tapestries, Bohemian engravings and Victorian travelogues, gleaning for any and all references to what the Gypsies wore. We learn about various luxurious materials and items of the past: toga-like wrapping blankets, Italian silks, oriental cloths, and head-dresses including gold-embroidered bonnets and turbans, some with delicate veils attached.

Moving further forward through time, there are sections on gold jewellery – brooches, sovereigns and creole earrings – and *kushti chokkers*, especially the handmade dealer boots and Northampton brogues beloved of Traveller men. She mentions the tailor in Oxfordshire who drew the business of Romany men from hundreds of miles around, all in search of a custom suit so that not even a 'proper old rai mush' could say he had the same.

The book is wonderfully rounded off with an extensive Gallery of Juliet's evocative paintings, showing the changing fashions on display at the fairs from the mid-1980s up until recent years. This has been a trip down memory lane for me and I'm grateful for the ride.

Damian le Bas

# INTRODUCTION

*"He may best a man beguile in whom the man hath most credence."*
Gower 1393

Gypsies have been a mystery since time immemorial.

It is so often said that "of course they're not real Gypsies" simply because gaujos cannot distinguish between the genuine or the fake. This is because they are expected to remain old fashioned and fixed in time. In the same way, in the eyes of the public, a modern trailer does not carry the seal of authenticity, whereas a wagon does.

The paradox of the Gypsies is that they are both modern and old fashioned at the same time. They do not chuck out something, which is still useful or appeals, even though it is out of fashion. But this does not mean no change at all. The Gypsies change in a way that combines function and flamboyance.

Their trailers illustrate this paradox. Motorised, the Gypsies can now tow trailers with all the modern conveniences, which still match the splendour of the old highly decorated wagons. The stainless-steel gleams as did the gold-leaf, and the cut glass windows glitter like the Gypsies' crystal ball. The trailers have shape and style, and are embellished according to the owner's pocket. In fact they are no more like tourist caravans than peacocks are like battery hens.

In the sixteenth century Gypsies were accused of disguising themselves and of deceit, yet the accusers readily believed their tale that they were penitents from Egypt.

The line between a lie and a good story may be so fine that the one is barely discernible from the other. Not only must the story be recognised, but it should be understood that the Gypsies would have endangered themselves if they had told the truth at the time of their arrival in Europe. This has held true over the years.

The heart of the matter is that the Gypsies are a living contradiction. They have been travelling for at least nine hundred years, and for at least nine hundred years they have been acting a play – a mystery play acted in real life in front of a huge and hostile audience of gaujos. It is out of necessity that Gypsies became experts at both attracting and avoiding attention.

The illiterate, mediaeval Gypsies were more sophisticated than a modern advertising agent or public relations expert. They knew more about creating and sustaining an image than a film star, and this image was partly true and partly a cover up or disguise. Mystery, as much as their own language, was one of the Gypsies' weapons for survival. It enabled them to attract public attention when needed yet avoid it when danger threatened.

JJ

# SOURCES

## The Hunt for the Truth

Samuel Rid wrote in the Art of Juggling 1612, that, *"there arrived in Southern England c1529 certain Egyptians, who being excellent in quaint tricks & devizes, not known here at that time amongst us, were esteemed & held in great admiration, for what with their strange attire & garments, together with their slights & legerdermains, they were spoke of far & near."*

The task of unravelling a 'Mystery,' complicated by hostility, romanticism and ignorance, is not easy. Despite being spoken of far and wide, contemporary references, written during the Gypsies' travels West, are few and usually as scanty as Rid's. The illustrative material presents another problem, that of accuracy. It is clear that not all artists actually saw their subjects in real life, making scrutiny vital, especially when art inclined towards romanticism.

Accounts drawn from Literature provide another source of information requiring the same scrutiny, and it was not until the nineteenth century that there was a burst of reliable interest. The Gypsy Lore Society founded in 1888 was a result of this interest. The Society's Journals, which were published well into the twentieth century, are rich in the affairs of 'Little Egypt' and contain thoroughly researched articles either drawn from the past or contemporary to their time. I am hugely indebted to those faithful, enthusiastic members, who provided such a wealth of valuable material.

August 17th 1427, there arrived at Paris, a dozen of Penancers, (doers of penance) as they called themselves, to wit, a Duke, a Count, and ten others, all on horseback, who pretended to be very good Christians, and that they were of the Lower Egypt. They said farther, that not a very long time before, the Christians had conquered them & their whole country, and had made them all turn Christians, or put to death those that would not. That the Lords among them, who were baptized, were made masters of the country, as they had been before; that they promised to be good & loyal Christians, and to preserve their faith in Jesus Christ, as long as they lived; and that they had a King & Queen in their country, who lived within their own manors. But they said, that a little while after they had embraced the Christian faith, the Saracens came and attacked them, and as they were not well fixed in the Christian faith, they made very little resistance, as in duty to their country they were bound to do, but submitted to the enemy, became Saracens, as before, and renounced their faith in Jesus Christ. That upon this, many of them left their native country, & came to settle among the Christians; but it happened afterwards, that when the Christian Princes, such as the Emperor of Germany, the King of Poland, and others, heard how their countrymen had so treacherously deserted the Christian Faith, and so readily become

Saracens & Idolaters, they fell upon them, with a view either to drive them out of their country, or to make Christians of such of them as were not: And at last in a great Council it was resolved, by the Emperor, & other Princes, that they could not suffer them to remain in their territories, without the consent of the Pope; whereupon they were ordered to repair to the Holy Father at Rome. That all of them, both small & great, went thither with great difficulty, especially to the children. When they were there, they made a general confession of their sins; and when the Pope heard their confession, after mature deliberation in his Council, he ordered them, as a penance, to wander for seven years together through the World, without ever lying in a bed; and that they might have some way to support themselves, he ordered, as they said, that every Bishop and mitred Abbot should give them a charity of ten livres, as was mentioned in the letters, with which he furnished them, to the Bishops of the Church: Then, after he had given them his blessing, they departed, and had been wandering for five years through the World before they arrived at Paris.

The before-mentioned twelve, says the Author, arrived at Paris on the 17th of August, 1427, & on the day of John the Baptist's Decollation, (Aug. 29th) the whole body of their common people arrived. These were not suffered to enter Paris, but were, by the Magistrates, lodged in the Chapel of St. Denys, & were, in the whole, but about 100, or six score of men, women & children. When they left their country they were, as they said, about 1000 or 1200, but the rest had died by the way; and their King & Queen, they said, were still alive, and were still in hopes of having a settlement in this World; for that the Pope had promised to give them a good & fertile country to inhabit; but that they must first sincerely finish the period of their penance. Whilst they were at the Chapel, there were never seen such crowds of people at any fair or public festival, as resorted to see them from Paris, St Denys, & all the places round. Almost all, or by far the greatest part of them, had their ears bored, and a silver ring, some two, in each ear; which, they said was the fashion in their country. The men were very black, with their hair frizzled: The women were the most ugly, & the blackest that were ever seen; almost all had their heads uncovered, with hair as black as a horse's tail; and for clothes, they had nothing but a single garment or shift, tied upon the shoulder with a linen string or cord, & a short cloak. In short, they were the poorest creatures that had ever been seen in France; and yet, notwithstanding their poverty, they had sorceresses amongst them, who by looking into people's hands, pretended to tell them all that had, or would happen to them; by which they sowed contention in several families; for they often told the husband, ·

'Thy wife has played thee a slippery trick.' But what was worse, while they were thus telling people their fortunes, either by magic art, or by the help of the Devil, or by slight of hand, they drew, as I was told, the money out of people's pockets into their own. 'Tis true, I went myself three or four times to talk with them, but never saw them look into anyone's hand, nor did I lose anything. But this was what the people everywhere reported; insomuch, that at last an account of it reached the Bishop of Paris, who went thither, carrying along with him a famous preacher called the Little Jacobin, and he, by the Bishop's order, after preaching a fine sermon, excommunicated all those who showed them their hands, or put any faith in their predictions; and at last, being ordered away, they departed on the festival of the Nativity of the Virgin Mary, (Sept. 8) taking their route towards Pontoise.'

This is the account given by the author of this Journal, and as the Journal is authentic, it shows the falsehood of the vulgar opinion, that our Gypsies are the same with, or are descended from the people called Zinganees in Turkey, who were banished from Egypt after the Sultan Selimus had conquered that Kingdom in 1517. The story these people told at Paris was certainly a fiction, contrived to impose upon the superstition & ignorance of that age; and yet there was some foundation in history for a part of it; for in the 13th century, the

Lower Egypt had been conquered by Louis IX of France, who very probably forced the people he conquered to turn Christians; but he did not long hold his conquest, for being defeated & taken prisoner by the Saracens, he was obliged to give up all his conquests & return home: How ever, I doubt much if any number of people left Egypt at that time on account of their religion; because if they had, they would have come directly to France, when that King returned with the remains of his army, and not have wandered through all Asia Minor, Greece, Hungary, Poland and Germany.

For this reason I am more apt to join in opinion with those who think that our Gypsies are the descendants of the people called Uxians by the Byzantine historians, who from Persia spread themselves all over Mysia, & lived chiefly by telling people their fortunes: The character of our European Gypsies being the same with that given by ancient historians to that people, viz. Quos aliena juvant, propriis habitare molestum; and their way of supporting themselves here is the same with that practised by their ancestors in Asia; it is very natural to suppose, that some of these old fortune-tellers got themselves wafted over the Hellespoint from Mysia into Greece, and their first appearing in Poland, Bohemia, (from whence they are by the French called Bohemians) & the Eastern parts of Germany, is a confirmation of this supposition.

Their pretending to be Egyptians, who had left their country for the sake of their religion, when it was conquered by the Saracens, was a story well calculated for gaining a favourable reception from the Grecian Emperor, and other Christian princes; but their pilferings & idleness has since produced severe laws against them in most countries of Europe.

I am, &c.

This account from an old French Journal and written by Pasquin
was included in a letter to the London Magazine, 1747

# 1 EASTERN ORIGINS

## First Impressions

In the year 1417 the inhabitants of Hanover, Holstein and Mecklenbourg were amazed by the arrival of strangers, who were described as very dirty, very ugly and as black as Tartars. Some rode on horseback – others walked.

Who were those dark people who arrived in Arras in 1421 – the men whose faces were scarcely visible for their bushy beards and long black hair, and who wore extraordinary

dress; whose women wrapped cloth around their heads, like turbans, and wore cloth shirts slit in front exposing the breasts, under blankets of coarse woollen fabric attached to the shoulders, and whose children like their mothers had rings in their ears and were wrapped in these blankets?

Who were these strangers whose superbly dressed chiefs had hunting dogs like the nobility and whose women, children and baggage were drawn in wagons – the women described as wearing chemises that barely covered, and earrings and much other finery?

Were they Egyptians as the troupe, who arrived in Bologna in 1422, led by their Chief Micehel or Michael of Egypt, called themselves?

How true was the tale, which Pasquin recorded when he described the arrival in Paris of a dozen penancors – a Duke, a Count and ten others – all on horseback and the forerunners of yet another group of about one hundred?  Clearly they were the same race.  Who else would wear two rings in each ear?  What other men had been seen with frizzled hair?  What other women would wear single garments or shifts tied on the shoulder with linen cord, and unusual short cloaks?

Like Micehel, these strangers said they were from lower Egypt, and their story was full of drama.  Conquered in their own country by the Christians, they adopted the Christian faith to avoid certain death.  A little while after, they were attacked by the Saracens, who forced those wishing to remain in their country to renounce the Christian faith and become Saracens.  When this treachery became known amongst the Christians, it was resolved that these strangers should not remain in their territories without consent from the Pope.  So with great difficulty they travelled to Rome to make a confession, resulting in the Pope's order that as a penance they should wander seven years without ever lying in a bed, but receive from the Bishops and Abbots a charity of ten livres to help support themselves.

Their tale has long been pondered and George Borrow doubtless drew the right conclusion.  He thought the tale probably originated amongst the priests and learned men of Eastern Europe, who startled by the sudden incursion of strangers, foreign in appearance and language, skilled in divination and the occult arts, tried to find a clue to such a phenomenon in the Scriptures resulting in the transformation of the Roma (Gypsies) of Hindustan into Egyptian penitents, the name since borne.

Borrow was a leading authority on Gypsies.  Furthermore, he slept in the open with them so his knowledge was both intimate and intellectual.

He realized only too well that people could be forced into romanticizing.

It is hardly surprising that the fifteenth century Europeans readily accepted that these strange visitors were 'dukes of lower Egypt' for then few knew what was going on in the next county or province, and for most people Western contact with Egypt was little more than our contact with outer space today.

Now we know that the Gypsies originated in India and began their departure before the year AD 1000, and that circa 1100, they were recorded at Mount Athos. Therefore, their migration was during the period of the Crusades. But the experiences of the Crusaders, early pilgrims and travellers, who visited Egypt after 1400, would have made little, if any impact on the ordinary Western European. Only a few of the intelligentsia would have benefited from their accounts. After all, the fact that contact existed between Italy and Mamluk Egypt, that Italian merchants used to call frequently at Eastern Mediterranean ports and that an exchange of embassies was not uncommon, had not prevented the Pope from being taken in! The fact that the supreme pontiff found this story credible was even more significant than the prevalent ignorance of the time. His papal injunction secured the Gypsies the respect of clergy and laity alike, enabling them to follow their nomadic inclinations.

An article of 1861 suggested 'great cunning' and tact was used in devising and executing a scheme to secure a hospitable reception. I agree with Walter Simson who attributed this to 'high intelligence'. He claimed that on their arrival in Britain, the Gypsies – having hobnobbed with all classes of society, including the highest, on their travels West – were far more intelligent and sophisticated that the average country person. The fact that the 'story' may have been put into their heads by the clergy, as Borrow suggested, does not diminish the Gypsies' acumen but underlines their wisdom in utilizing it to gain entry to the countries on their route. Name dropping and letters of introduction are still used today!

By 1562, as the Act CAP XX [see overleaf] shows, the 'Mysterious People' had thoroughly mystified the Western Europeans. This Act, preceded and followed by others, attempted to clarify who they were by making it an offence to disguise themselves or pretend to be Egyptians by their dress. Certainly it would have been no advantage to anyone who

4

# CAP XX An Act for further Punishment of Vagabonds, calling themselves Egyptians

Whereas since the Act made in the first & second years of the late King Philip & Queen Mary, for the punishment of that false & subtle company of vagabonds calling themselves Egyptians, there is a scruple & doubt risen, whether such persons as being born within this realm of England, or other the Queen Highness's dominions, and are or shall become of the fellowship or company of the said vagabonds, by transforming or disguising themselves in their apparel, or in a certain counterfeit speech or behaviour, are punishable by the said Act in like manner as others of that sort are being strangers born, & transported into this realm of England:

11 Therefore for the avoiding of all doubts and ambiguities in that behalf, and to the intent that all such sturdy & false vagabonds of that sort, living only upon the spoil of the simple people, may be condignly met withal and punished, (2) Be it enacted by the Queen our Sovereign Lady, the Lords spiritual & temporal, and the Commons in this present Parliament assembled, & by the authority of the same, That the said statute made in the first & second years of the said late King & Queen concerning those vagabonds calling themselves Egyptians,

THE STAT. OF 1&2 P2/M. C4 CONCERNING EGYPTIANS SHALL CONTINUE IN FORCE

shall continue, remain and be in full force, strength
& effect.

III And yet moreover, be it enacted by the authority aforesaid, that all and every person and
persons, which from and after the first day of
May now next ensuing, shall be seen or found
within this realm of England or Wales, in
any company or fellowship of vagabonds,
commonly called, or calling themselves Egyptians, or counterfeiting, transforming or disguising
themselves by their apparel, speech or other behaviour,
like unto such vagabonds, commonly called or calling themselves Egyptians, & so shall or do continue &
remain in the same, either at one time, or at several
times by the space of one month: That they the said
person or persons, shall by virtue of this Act be
deemed & judged a felon & felons; (2) and shall therefore suffer pains of death, loss of lands & goods, as in
cases of felony by the order of the common laws of this
realm: (3) and shall upon the trial of them, or any
of them therein, be tried in the county, and by the inhabitants of the county or place where they or he shall
be apprehended or taken, and not per medietatatum
linguae; (4) and shall lose the privilege & benefit of
sanctuary and clergy.

IT SHALL BE
FELONY FOR
EGYPTIANS
OR OTHERS
COUNTER·
FEITING
THEMSELVES
LIKE TO THEM
TO REMAIN
A MONTH
IN THIS
REALM

IV Provided always, and be it enacted by the
authority aforesaid, that this Act shall not

TO WHAT
PERSONS
THIS ACT
SHALL NOT
EXTEND

in any wise extend to any child or children being
within the age of fourteen years, nor to any of
the said persons being in prison the last day of this
present parliament, so that he or they so being in
prison, do within fourteen days next after his or
their delivery out of prison, either depart out of this
realm of England & Wales, or put him or themselves
to some honest service, or exercise some lawful work,
trade, or occupation, and utterly forsake the said
idle & false trade, conversation & behaviour of the
said counterfeit & disguised vagabonds, commonly
called, or calling themselves Egyptians.

V. Provided also, & be it enacted by the authority aforesaid, that the said Act made in the
first & second years of the said late King &
Queen, shall not extend to compel any person or persons born within any the Queen Majesty's
dominions, to depart out of this realm of England or
Wales, but only to bind them and every of them to leave
their said naughty, idle & ungodly life & company, and
to place themselves in some honest service, or to exercise themselves at home with their parents, or elsewhere honestly in some lawful work, trade or occupation; anything mentioned in this said former Act to
the contrary hereof in any wise notwithstanding.

NONE
BORN IN
THE REALM
COMPELL-
·ABLE TO
DEPART
THENCE

was not a Gypsy to pretend to be one since already they were severely legislated against. And it is unlikely anyone would have successfully counterfeited their dark physical appearance. Further confusion was probably caused by the established Gypsies and other travelling people, fearful of their already difficult life becoming impossible, denying that fresh incursions were also Gypsies.

The legislation encouraged the Gypsies to adopt a more conventional form of dress in Britain at least, in order that they could continue to live as they wished, without interference from the Authorities. But no Acts could remove the doubt and ambiguity surrounding the so-called Egyptians simply by ordering the removal of their disguising apparel – indeed they probably exacerbated the confusion, especially as most Western Europeans did not know what Egyptians looked like, let alone counterfeits.

Taken from 'The Haywain' central panel of a triptych by Jerome Bosch 1450-1516 one of the earliest paintings to represent the Gypsies Museum of Prado, Madrid

When the Gypsies first appeared in Europe, some were shabbily dressed, while others were finely dressed. They wore turbans, rings in their ears and much other finery. Mediaeval man was used to seeing both great richness and extreme poverty of dress, but not within the same group. And this together with their dark colouring must have been an extraordinary sight for Europeans at that time. The effect was not so much what was worn, but how it was worn and by whom it was worn.

llustration to the section 'De improbe mendicantibus' from Brandt's Navis stultifera (Basilee, 1507) p. lviii'

In the second half of the fifteenth and the sixteenth century references are made to 'a peculiar style of headdress.' This was the turban, which was an important item because, to the Europeans, it seemed to symbolise the Gypsies' Egyptian origin, although it might have come from India or other countries. The poet John Skelton (circa 1517) describes the wonderful headdress of Elynour Rumminge, likening it to that of an Egyptian. And about this time the Gypsies' dress was also considered theatrical enough for plays and Court Mummeries; Edward Hall, in his Chronicle of King Henry VIII, described a Court Mummery in 1510 and wrote that two ladies had 'their heades rouled in pleasauntes (lawn or gauze) and typpers (brims of caps or bonnets) like the Egyptians, embroidered with gold.' He also wrote that at a State Banquet in 1520 'there entered into the chamber eight ladies tired (with head-dresses) like the Egipcians very richly.'

Generally there was a time-lag between the Gypsies' tale and the Gypsies' guise and for this reason it seems more than likely that the adoption of certain items of clothing was deliberate to give credence to the tale. This was by no means difficult. Asian costume had already

Adapted from the illustration above left to the section 'De improbe
mendicantibus' showing a gaujo woman wearing a pleated cloak
and kerchief of the same period - early C16

been introduced into Eastern Europe in the fourteenth and fifteenth
centuries and then penetrated Western and Central Europe. In addition,
the sea traffic, which, since the Crusades, brought Oriental produce to
Europe, remained active. Therefore, Oriental materials, decoration and
forms were introduced into Europe just as the Gypsies were introducing
themselves and travelling across the continent.

Not only were sumptuous costume materials imported into Western Europe, but their manufacture began in certain regions of Spain and Italy. At the beginning of the sixteenth century there was an enormous Italian output of various silk textiles. At the same time much more colour was used due to the provision of new tints and the fact that use of colours in dress was no longer restricted by their former symbolic meaning. Varied armorial motifs were used as well, including stripes, chequerboard or figures. Despite this activity in Europe, Oriental cloths continued to be imported into Western Europe and were used for luxury garments such as those worn for ceremonial entries of Princes or sovereigns. Although silk was so popular, it did not supplant linen or wool.

From an engraving of Gypsy Family from the 'Master of Cabinet of Amsterdam' End of CXV Bibliotheque National, Paris

From a drawing in a collection of sixteenth century portraits Bibliotheque Municipale, Arras

From the fifteenth century Italian weavers, whilst retaining traces of Oriental influence in their decorative repertory, enlarged their own floral motifs to unusual dimensions, decorating their embossed velvets with large pomegranates or thistles set between wide wavy lines.

In view of the Oriental influences, it is no surprise that the turban was introduced into fashionable dress in the fifteenth century. Mainly worn by women, it was either padded or softly loose and decorated by a veil or liripipe, or both. When at the height of fashion in about 1440-1450, men adopted it too.

The turban was particularly worn in countries in central and Eastern Europe where it may have been first encountered and adopted by the Gypsies.

It is understandable and obvious that the Gypsies had to use past and current events to fabricate a story ingenious enough to secure a hospitable reception wherever they went. Once sumptuous materials and extravagant head-dresses were readily at hand, the Gypsies were able to make their own ceremonial entries as 'Lords, Dukes and Counts of Lower Egypt.' It was not the dress itself, which made their entries so spectacular, but the contrast of luxury and poverty. Additionally, and more importantly, Gypsies are striking in themselves, and not strikingly ugly as contemporary descriptions suggest! Although it has to be appreciated that at the time pale complexions were considered to be beautiful – to be dark and hairy did not. Western men were clean shaven and wore their hair short and 'unfrizzled,' cut like a pudding basin, and the fashionable women went so far as shaving their heads so that no hair, or very little showed beneath their turbans.

In those days people were conventionally poor or conventionally fashionable – the Gypsies were neither. An ordinary article of clothing might have appeared extraordinary on one of them, simply because it was worn in an unexpected way.

Although there is a strong argument that the Gypsies developed their guise to give credence to their story of origin, it must also have been influenced by their own innate taste. They have a natural flair for the flamboyant and for self-ornament, not out of vanity but an inner need. And this tendency was doubtless developed and enhanced by their stop in the Byzantine Empire on their route from India. The Gypsy style is both an expression of, and a means of, preserving the Gypsy spirit. They use colour and dazzle to keep up their spirits, and this distinctive flamboyant style has helped them to survive the hardships of their difficult history.

Fortunately, the fashion in Europe at the time of their arrival could be adapted to suit the 'story' as well as suiting their taste and it was available. Then as now, they were not slaves to fashion but adopted whatever appealed to them. That is why this period is so important, because it established their taste, which, unlike that of gaujos, has remained constant.

Centuries later some Gypsies believed the story of their forbears. A very intelligent Gypsy informed James Simson that his race sprung from a body of men – a cross between the Arabs and Egyptians – that left in the wake of the Jews. And in the last century the late Gordon Boswell in his autobiography confirmed his belief that his forefathers came from Egypt, and that the information was handed down from his Grandfather

Wester, to his Father, to himself. Paradoxically this shows that the romantic story might have a grain of truth after all. Certainly it proves the tenacity of the Gypsies' oral tradition.

After La Zingara by Boccacino
(1501-1546)  Musee des Offices,
Florence

## II EASTERN ORIGINS

### Sixteenth Century Dress in Europe

The Gypsies brought from India three characteristics: a conservatism or traditionalism, a love of jewellery and a partiality to bright colour – and four specific items; the women's scarf, the diklo (neckerchief) worn by men, the blanket for both sexes and the women's intricate plaited hair-styles and preference for long hair. It is the first characteristic – conservatism – inherent in British and other Gypsies that has preserved all the others.

Dar, an Indian costume historian, said 'In India, the use of ornaments as an indication of wealth is so common that, except in cases where it's guided by well-cultivated taste, the extravagant over-ornamentation tends to defeat the very purpose it was intended to serve. An Indian lady has often been humorously described as a peripatetic mine of precious metals.' He also said that 'ornamentation is the sartorial heritage of Ancient India.' Dar might have been writing of the Gypsies.

The scarf, which has been continuously worn by Gypsy women in varying ways, must surely have its roots in India, where it has been a constituent of women's dress since Vedic times.

The dress of the Brahmin men consisted of a squat turban, the dhoti for the lower part of the body and the scarf thrown over the shoulder without covering the body. This scarf is most probably the origin of the diklo, which one might say became the hallmark of a Gypsy man from the eighteenth century.

Another important survival, due to the Gypsies' innate conservatism, is the intricate plaited hairstyle, as seen in the Gothic tapestries of Tournai.

The Gypsy blanket, which was often striped, is well illustrated by the Egyptien and Egyptienne, Sebastian Münster's Gypsy Family and the Cingara Orientale. Jean Brodeau (1500-63) [see overleaf] described the blanket as resembling a Roman toga. But since the toga was semi-circular and the illustrations clearly show square corners, these blankets more closely resemble the himation of ancient Greece. The shawls and mantles (chadars) of India are similar wrapping garments and Dar thinks

Zugineuner from Münster's 'Cosmographi univer-salis' 1554 Basel

The Egyptien and the Egyptienne from an engraving from 'Recueil de la diversité des habits'by Francois Deprez (Paris 1567) Bibliothèque nationale Paris

Cingara Orientale from Cesare Vecellio 'Degli Habiti anticha et moderni' Venetia 1590

they might have been introduced into the country during the Greek Conquests. These garments, like the Gypsy blanket, were a useful protection against the rain as well as serving as bedding.

The cloak or himation was a large four-cornered piece of woollen cloth, which was thrown over the left shoulder or the left arm. The fact that illustrations such as Hans Weigel's show it worn over the right arm may be due to the fact that they are engravings, or because Gypsies are not bound by convention. This garment usually reached to the knee or a little lower – to wear it too long was considered a sign of extravagance or pride. This becomes an interesting analogy, when one sees the lengths of similar garments worn by the Gypsies, who are neither ashamed of extravagance nor of being proud.

So it is possible that the Gypsies, in wearing the blanket, reintroduced to Europe an ancient Greek mode of dress, which was originally introduced to India by Alexander the Great.

It is less likely that the Gypsies introduced the chlamys and the conventional high turban from India into mediaeval Europe. The chlamys was yet another wrapping garment like that worn by the Gypsy in Bordone's painting 'Rest during flight into Egypt'. The Roman chlamys was semi-circular, fastening on the right shoulder or in front by a buckle or fibular. It passed into Byzantine dress and was worn in Europe for sports and travelling purposes for a long time after. The Gypsies showed a preference for the side fastening, which was not in common use in Europe at that time – so a common garment uncommonly worn.

After Paris Bordone's 'Rest during flight into Egypt' circa 1558
Musée des Beaux Arts, Strasbourg

Unlike the origin of the blanket, that of the chlamys is less clear. Although it could have been adopted in India, it is more probable that it was adopted when the Gypsies reached Byzantium.

From a miniature given to Paris
in 1590  Bibliothèque nationale

From the Sermon of St. John the Baptist by Pieter
Bruegel 1566 Musée des Beaux-arts, Budapest

The same question hangs over the turban, which could have been brought from India or readopted in mediaeval Europe, where it became fashionable. Gypsies are first mentioned as wearing it in 1421 and definitely seem to have worn it into the seventeenth century, long after it ceased to be fashionable with non Gypsies. They did not conform to fashion either, by usually allowing their hair to show, unlike the Europeans. This use of the turban illustrates the Gypsies' innate conservatism, as well as their mastery of the art of selective borrowing, skilfully choosing those items of local dress, which are closest to their own ancient traditions.

One item of Gypsy dress, for which there is no prototype, re-mains a mystery – the Bern. Both Breugel's Gypsy woman and the Cingara Orientale wear this flat turban, which was described by Vecellio as a diadem made of light wood, covered with many arm-length bands of cloth. The name Bern is also included in the Gypsy vocabulary obtained by Joseph Justus Scaliger (1540-1609), where it is translated 'rota fascilis involuta, quam capiti imponunt mulieres Nubianae' – a wheel wound round with bands, which the Nubian, i.e. Gypsy women place on the head. It remains to be proved that this head-dress was ever worn in Nubia, or by Nubians with whom the Gypsies might have come into contact on their migration. With or without this proof, the adoption of the Bern seems to indicate that the Gypsies were motivated by aesthetic reasons rather than ulterior motives. Gypsies dressed flamboyantly because they were Gypsies, not because they wished to be regarded as Lords and Ladies of Lower Egypt.

While an unusual item of dress at this time, the striped blanket was evidently popular with the Gypsies. See also the Serie de Carrabarra, seventeen tapestries from Tournai made in the first third of the C16, probably in the workshops of Arnold Poissonnier. Chapter III

# CAP IV. An Act against certain Persons calling themselves Egyptians

Where in a Parliament holden at Westminster in the xxij year of the reign of our late Sovereign Lord King Henry the Eigth, ( for the avoiding and banishing out of this realm of certain out landish people calling themselves Egyptians, using no craft nor feat of merchandises for to live by, but going from place to place in great companies, using great, subtle and crafty means to deceive the King's subjects, bearing them in hand, that they by palmistry could tell men's & women's fortune, and so many times by craft and subtlety deceive the people of their money, & committed divers great & heinous felonies & robberies, to the great hurt & deceit of the people ); (2) It was a mongst other things then enacted, that from the time of the making of the said Act no such persons should be suffered to come within this the King's realm, upon pain of forfeiture to the King of all their goods & chattels, and they to be commanded to avoid the realm within fifteen days next after the commandment, upon pain of imprisonment; (3) and such persons calling themselves Egyptians, as were then within this realm, should depart within six teen days next after proclamation of the said Act, upon pain of imprisonment, and forfeiture of all

PUNISHMENT FOR BRINGING EGYPTIANS INTO THIS REALM, &C. 22 H8.c.10 ENFORCED & EXPLAINED BY 5 EL. c.20 3 INST.102

their goods & chattels, with divers other clauses & articles contained in the said Act, as by the said Act more at large it appeareth : (4) Forasmuch as divers of the said company, and such other like persons, not fearing the penalty of the said Stat. ute, have enterprised to come over again into this realm, using their old, accustomed devilish and naughty practices & devices, with such abomina. ble living as is not in any Christian realm to be permitted, named or known, and be not only pun. ished for the same, to the perilous & evil example of our Sovereign Lord & Lady the King & Queen Majesties' most loving subjects, and to the utter & extreme undoing of divers and many of them, as evidently doth appear :

11 For reformation whereof, be it ordained & enact. ed by the King & Queen our Sovereign Lord and Lady, the Lords spiritual & temporal, and the Commons in this present Parliament ass. embled, and by the authority of the same, that if any person or persons after the last day of January next coming do willingly transport, bring or convey into this realm of England or Wales, any such per. sons calling themselves, or commonly called Egypt. ians, that they he or they so transporting, bringing or conveying in any such person, contrary to the true meaning of this Act, shall forfeit & lose for every

THE PENALTY FOR BRINGING OF EGYPTIANS INTO THIS REALM

time so offending, forty pounds of lawful money of England.

III And be it further enacted by the authority aforesaid, that if any of the said persons called Egyptians, which shall be transported & conveyed into this realm of England or Wales, as is aforesaid, do continue & remain within the same by the space of one month, that they he or they so offending shall by virtue of this Act be deemed & judged a felon & felons, (2) and shall therefore suffer pains of death, loss of lands & goods, as in cases of felony, by order of the common law of this realm, (3) and shall upon the trial of them or any of them therein so tried in the county, and by the inhabitants of the county or place where they or he shall be apprehended or taken, and not per medietatem linguae, (4) and shall lose the benefit & privilege of sanctuary & clergy.

IT SHALL BE FELONY FOR EGYPTIANS TO REMAIN IN ENGLAND A MONTH

IV And be it further enacted by the authority aforesaid, that if the Egyptians, or other persons commonly calling themseles Egyptians, & every of them now being within this realm of England or Wales, do not depart out of the same within xx days next after proclamation of this present Act shall be made, that they he or they which shall not depart within the said time, according to the true meaning of this Act, shall

THE PENALTY FOR THE EGYPTIANS THAT NOW BE TO TARRY IN ENGLAND

22

forfeit ⁊ lose all his ⁊ their goods ⁊ chattels, and
that then it shall be lawful to all ⁊ every the King's
⁊ Queen's subjects to seize the same; the one moiety
thereof to be to the use of our Sovereign Lord ⁊ Lady,
the King ⁊ Queen, and the other moiety thereof to
be to the use of him or them that shall so seize the

V And be it also enacted by the authority
aforesaid, that if the Egyptians, and other
persons commonly called Egyptians, ⁊ every
of them now being within this realm of England or
Wales, do not depart out ⁊ from the same within xl
days next after the proclamation shall be made of
this Act, that they he or they which shall not depart ⁊
avoid within the said time of xl days, according to
the true meaning of this Act, shall be judged ⁊ deemed according to the laws of this realm of England,
a felon ⁊ felons, and shall suffer therefore pains of
death, loss of lands ⁊ goods, as in other cases of felony,
and shall be tried as is aforesaid, and without having
any benefit or privilege of sanctuary or clergy.

THE PENALTY
FOR EGYPTIANS
NIX TO DE·
PART WITHIN
FORTY DAYS

VI And be it further enacted by the authority
aforesaid, that if any person after the first
day of January next coming, shall sue for the
obtaining of any licence, letter or passport,
for any of the said persons called Egyptians to abide
or continue within this realm of England or Wales,
contrary to the tenor of this Act, that then every such
person so suing shall forfeit ⁊ lose for the same xl

THE PENALTY
FOR SUING OE
LICENCE FOR
EGYPTIANS
TO TARRY IN
ENGLAND

florins of lawful money of England; (2) and that every such licence, letter or passport shall be by virtue of this Act void to all intents and purposes; (3) the one moiety of all which sums of money to be forfeited as is aforesaid, shall be to the King & Queen our Sovereign Lord & Lady, and the other moiety thereof to be to him or them that will sue for the same in any court of record, by action of debt, bill, plaint or information, wherein no essoin, wager of law, nor protection shall be admitted or allowed.

VII Provided always, and be it enacted by the authority aforesaid, that this present Act, nor anything therein contained, shall not extend or be hurtful to any of the said persons commonly called Egyptians, which within the said time of xx days next after the said proclamation to be made as is aforesaid, shall leave that naughty, idle & ungodly life & company, and be placed in the service of some honest & able inhabitant or inhabitants within this realm, or that shall honestly exercise himself in some lawful work or occupation, but that he or they so continuing in service, or other lawful work or occupation, shall (during such time as he or they shall so continue) be discharged of all pains & forfeitures contained in this Act.

A PROVISO FOR EGYPTIANS. WHICH LEAVE THEIR NAUGHTY TRADE

service, or other lawful work or occupation, shall (during such time as he or they shall so continue) be discharged of all pains & forfeitures contained in this Act.

VIII Provided also, and be it enacted by the authority aforesaid that this Act shall not in any wise extend to any child or children, being not above the age of thirteen years, nor to any of the said persons being now in prison, so that he or they so being in prison do depart out of this realm within fourteen days next after his or their delivery out of prison; (2) nor shall extend to charge any manner of person or persons as accessary to any offence or offences contained or specified in this Statute.

From Carrying the Cross, Tournai Tapestry, Château d'Angers

# III ACROSS THE SEA

## Sixteenth and Seventeenth Centuries

The earliest authentic notice, so far discovered, of the Gypsies' first appearance in the British Isles is a letter from James IV of Scotland to the King of Denmark, dated 1506. Unfortunately, British sources provide scanty detail of the Gypsies' personal appearance in the sixteenth century, referring only to their disguise, and the next century is not much better. Therefore, the outlook would be bleak for those interested in their dress without help and information from continental sources. This reliance is justifiable because the Gypsies retained a European link across the sea by successfully overcoming the legislation intended to prevent them from disembarking on British soil.

The legislation was indeed a formidable obstacle. Henry VIII enacted that 'on the importation of any such Egyptians, he, the importer, shall forfeit forty pounds for every trespass.' The legislation became even more severe in 1554 and it was not until 1856, under the Repeal of Obsolete Statutes Act, that the Gypsies could lawfully enter Britain.

How could this barrier have been broken?

The answer is found in the Gypsies' ingenious nature. Their flair for disguising themselves, combined with the fact there have always been those willing to flout the law for gain, meant the 1554 Act was not an insurmountable impediment. The flair is illustrated by Vidocq*, who recorded how, on the continent, they changed their clothes to avoid recognition.

'At break of day everybody was on foot, and the general toilet was made. But for their (the Gypsies) prominent features, their raven-black tresses, and oily and tanned skins, I should scarcely have recognised my companions of the preceding evening. The men, clad in rich jockey Holland vests, with leathern sashes like those worn by the men of Porsy, and the women, covered with ornaments of gold and silver, assumed the costume of Zealand peasants; even the children, whom I had seen covered with rags, were neatly clothed, and had an entirely different appearance. All soon left the house, and took different directions, that they might not reach the market place together, where the country people were assembled in crowds.'

*Eugene Francois Vidocq 1775-1887, principal agent to the French police 1795 joined a group of Gypsies. Memoirs - ghost written autobiography 1827

Vidocq had lodged all night with a band of Gypsies.

This picture closely resembles that given by Simson. He said in Scotland, the Gypsy youth, between ten and thirty years of age, formed bands with a captain at their head. The captains were well dressed and could not be taken for Gypsies. When they went to fairs they invariably went on horseback and never accompanied any of their men, who either travelled alone or in pairs. An old Gypsy told Simson that he had seen a principal chief (captain), dressed like a gentleman, travelling in a post-chaise for the purpose of attending fairs.

On the continent, during the Renaissance and into the seventeenth century, Gypsies continued to be a popular theme for artists, particularly in biblical scenes. Sometimes they were included in Egyptian landscapes because of their name, and another reason to depict them was the wide acceptance of various legends. For example, it was believed that Gypsies were condemned to perpetual wandering either because they had refused hospitality to the Holy Family, or that they had - if un-wittingly - forged the nails of the Crucifixion. In such scenes they were dressed like those Gypsies encountered by the artists in Europe.

The continental paintings confirm the written accounts and reveal even more clearly the Gypsies' love of exotic patterned fabrics, oriental in flavour, which were available and produced in Europe at this time.

Perhaps the most valuable early sixteenth century record is the Carrabarra series of tapestries from Tournai, which show the Gypsies alongside country-folk, ladies and gentlemen, or the well-off middle class, making immediate comparisons in their dress possible. Some of the men, who wear doublets and hose – the contemporary style – are only distinguishable from the gaujos by their swarthy complexion, beards and weapons, as well as their turbans, which are usually white. Others, obviously Gypsy in dress, wear short gowns, tunics or cloaks - mostly striped and braided. A mounted Gypsy in the 'Sale of the Children' wears a cloak with a fur collar reminiscent of the 'delia' of Eastern origin, although clasped at the side in Gypsy fashion. His head-dress is also exotic.

From the fifteenth century in Eastern Europe, 'vayvoydes' were appointed to manage and direct Gypsy groups. These appointments were made by the state and usually drawn from the nobility, seldom from the Gypsies themselves. The position was an honour and a reward, which carried benefits – one being the payment of an annual sum of money from each of the Gypsies under their leadership. These appointments must have significantly influenced the dress of the Gypsy men, many of whom appeared as much noblemen as Eastern. The mounted Gypsy already mentioned has the appearance of a leader, but - being bearded - he is clearly meant to represent a Gypsy. The Moors and Negroes appearing in these scenes should not be confused with the Gypsies with whom they were doubtless travelling.

The Gypsy women are dressed more characteristically than the men. Their long loose or plaited hair often shows from under their turbans and one woman wears a scarf draped over her head like an Indian. Most wear long robes of rich brocade or the stripes, so unusual for the time. Over these a number wear blankets, tied at one shoulder, or cloaks - again many striped. Some display their love of jewellery and all are barefoot. The children are barefoot too and either naked or scarcely covered by their dress, which resembles that of their elders. In one scene two little girls are shown dancing. One holds a bell in each hand and the other wears bells tied to her wrist and waist, a reminder of the kinkinis and ghungroos (anklets with bells) of ancient India. There is also reference to bells in England, in Thomas Dekker's 'Lanthorne and Candlelight' of 1609.

A drawing from part of a tapestry once held at the Château d' Effiat was included in Lacroix, 'Moeurs, usages et costumes au Moyen Age,' Paris 1871. Called Bohemiens en Marche, it was dated fifteenth century. However, Crofton throws doubt on this date believing the tapestry to be seventeenth century although the artist may have had some local knowledge of the Gypsies' visit to that part of France about 1420. The fact remains that their dress resembles that in the Tournai tapestries of the sixteenth century.

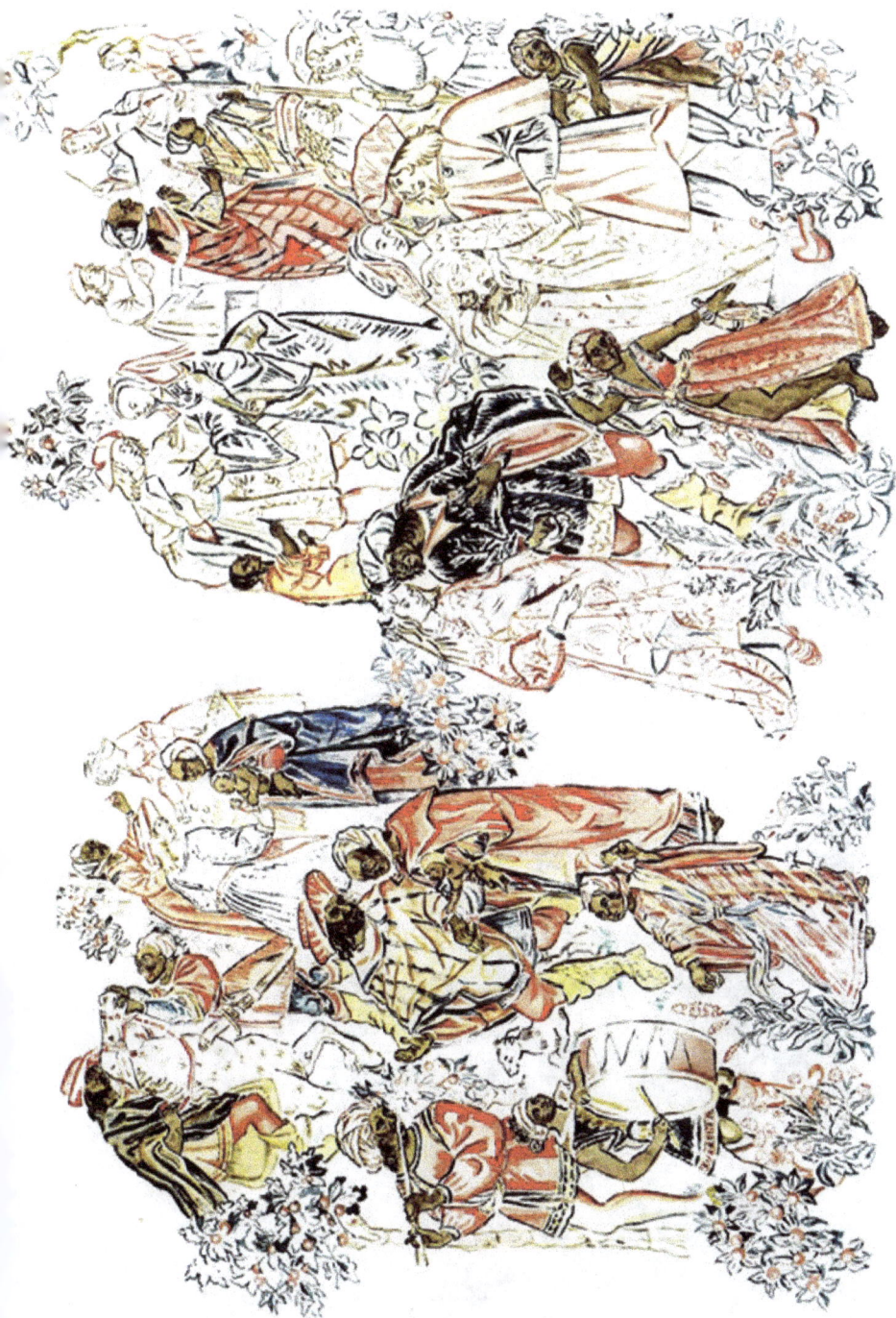

From a Country Fair Carrabarra series Tournai Tapestry Château de Gaasbeek circa 1501-25

From the Sale of the Children Carrabarra series Tournai Tapestry Château de Gaasbeek

Bohemiens en Marche from drawing of a fragment of tapestry said to be C15 (almost certainly later), which was included in Lacroix, Moeurs, usages et costumes au Moyen Age, Paris 1871

From a sixteenth century engraving by Lucas de Leyde of a Bohemien family from the Lowland. Collection F. Lugt, Institut Néerlandais, Paris These Gypsies prove that it is impossible to categorise their dress, for here it is humble compared to the flamboyance seen in the Tournai tapestries. It made sense for Gypsies travelling in a small family group to blend into their surroundings rather than draw attention to themselves.

English Gypsies from the Second Part of 'The Brave English Gipsie' circa 1630,
Roxburghe Ballads, Vol. III (Hertford 1875), British Library

A century later we see a very different dress from that in the Tournai tapestries. An illustration from 'The Brave English Gipsie', circa 1630, shows Gypsies in skins closely resembling the ancient kaunakes of the Sumerian civilization. These were fleece or goat-skins with long tufts of hair on the outside, and they continued in this form or in cloth, imitating skins, until well into the Middle Ages. For obvious reasons fleeces were normal clothing for shepherds. A mid fifteenth century French tapestry 'The Ball of the Savages' shows dancers wearing tufts of wool attached by pitch to close fitting garments. These dancers were not Gypsies, but Gypsies would have been aware of this form of dress. The 1630 illustration proves that this form of dress survived beyond the Middle Ages with Gypsies. Skins not only suited their style of living but at this period made an eminently suitable and necessary camouflage.

When the Gypsies first arrived in the British Isles their so called 'disguise' became a disguise in the modern sense of the word. Originally, as we have seen, the term was used by the gaujos referring to the strange and outlandish dress of the first Gypsies, who were doubtless simply wearing dress of Oriental or Eastern European character, in their own inimitable way.

However, the Gypsies had to alter their costume as a result of two different types of legislation. Sometimes they were ordered to dress like the local people, while at other times and places, it became an offence even to be a Gypsy and so they dressed like the locals to avoid detection. In the case their dress would have been a disguise as we understand it.

From a CVII Italian engraving
Bibliotheque National, Paris

The legislation, which made the Gypsies literally disguise themselves, was passed on both sides of the sea. Often in France, Spain, Portugal, Hungary and the Low Countries, the authorities ordered the Gypsies to dress like the local people. There was an order in 1673 by the Administrator of Provence, which obliged Gypsy women 'to lay aside their accustomed costume and to dress themselves like other women without assuming any distinction.' Gradually, as the legislation hardened, the women submitted and accepted the neutral tints and the banality of dress. Nevertheless, in lenient localities, the old traditional dress persisted longer, with modifications. For example, in Finland, as late as the end of the eighteenth century, the turban and a curious woollen shawl (chale), striped black, could be seen.

In Britain, legislation was to have a similar effect. The repressive Act of 1562, (quoted in full in Chapter I) CAP XX 'An Act for further punishment of Vagabonds, calling themselves Egyptians' referred to their 'transforming or disguising themselves in their apparel.' Moreover, it enacted that anyone seen or found within the realm in their company, or counterfeiting, transforming or disguising themselves by their apparel like such vagabonds would be deemed and judged a felon or felons, and therefore suffer pains of death, loss of lands and goods.

No wonder Gypsies abandoned the turban.

The Act of 1562 was not the first Act in England against the Gypsies, but it was the first to refer to their 'disguising apparel', which seems to have been so well known, that it was unnecessary to describe in detail.

Similar punitive measures were taken in Scotland. There was the Scottish Act of 1609 CAP XIII, which confirmed another of 1603, and commanded those 'commonly called Egyptians to leave the kingdom and never to return under pain of death.' The Act also made it lawful for Scottish subjects to apprehend, imprison, and execute to death the said Egyptians; and enacted that anyone receiving, supplying or entertaining any of the said Egyptians should lose their escheat, and be warded at the judge's will... Yet three years later, James VI was being forced to make bonds with clans of Gypsies throughout the kingdom! Furthermore, Scotsmen of respectability and influence protected the Gypsies and gave them shelter on their lands, after the promulgation of the cruel statute. However, since the Gypsies had no guarantee of finding protection, it was inevitable that the excessive severity of the sanguinary statute and the unrelenting manner in which it was often carried into effect would produce a great outward change in the Scottish Gypsies and cause them to discontinue wearing their recognizable dress.

The method the Gypsies used to acquire their new disguise was the same as before.

'These people, continuing about the country and practising their cozening art, purchased themselves great credit among the country people, and got much by palmistry and telling of fortunes; insomuch that they pitifully cozened poor country girls both of money, silver spoons, and the best of their apparel, or any goods they could make.' Samuel Rid.

If persuasion failed, they could, as before, resort to theft. A young Gypsy informed Simson that his forefathers considered it lawful, among themselves, to take from others, not of their own fraternity, anything they needed. Casting his eyes around the inside of Simson's house, he said: 'For instance were they to enter this room, they would carry off anything that could be of service to them, such as clothes, money, victuals, and c.' But, he added, 'all this proceeded from ignorance; they are now quite changed in their manners.'

Another Gypsy of about sixty years of age, told Simson that the Gypsies had a complete and thorough hatred of the whole community, excepting those who sheltered them or treated them kindly, and that a dexterous theft or robbery committed on any of the natives was looked upon as one of the most meritorious actions which a Gypsy could possibly perform.

Simson pointed out, and I must do the same, that at the time the Gypsies were no greater vagabonds, if as great, than many of the natives.

As the long history of the Gypsies grew even longer, so the difficulty of accounting for every aspect of their dress grows. Nevertheless, there is one constant factor - the unquenchable spirit of the Gypsies, expressed in the instinctive flamboyance and flair of their dress.

Part 1

Part 2

From an etching Bohemiens on the March by Jaques Callot 1592-1635, Bibliotheque Nationale, Paris. The success of the Gypsies in blending into the local scene, and in adapting local dress to their own needs, is clear from the statements of Vidocq and Simson. The conventional dress is illustrated, along with their unconventional berns, scarves and blankets, in Callot's depictions. It is particularly interesting to compare the Gypsy leaders described by Simson with these illustrated by Callot. It is equally interesting to consider the grandeur of the dress, which must have been worn by the vayvodes (leaders), selected by the King from the nobility to lead, advise and extract annual taxes from the Gypsies. This was the situation when the Gypsies first roamed Europe, and in time, when the vayvodes were no longer crown appointments, the Gypsies continued the custom among themselves, choosing their own leaders. The distinguishing mark of dignity was a large whip hanging over the shoulder - still an important accessory for the men today.

Jean-Paul Clèebert wrote of Callot that "In the seventeenth century, nobody understood the Gypsies better than the French painter and engraver, Jacques Callot. He is known to have lived with them. His engravings have the precision of ethnographic documents."

From a tapestry woven in the second half of the C17, probably at Lille. Gypsies were a popular subject after Teniers scenes, among the C17-C18 Brussels and early C18 English Soho weavers.To impress and attract her customers, the fortune-teller wears a provocative short skirt and flamboyant flat turban, and overskirt or pinnie tucked into her belt, as country people did at the time.The young pickpocket is also dressed for the job, in a doublet not unlike that of the man whose pocket he picks. His clothes are worn with typical abandon - his oversized shirt showing beneath his breeches. The mother wears a kerchief edged with two red stripes, or a linen hat, either un-usually worn. Her baby is carried attached to her back by a shawl, a practice not entirely peculiar to Gypsies, but more commonly used by them and for a longer time. The young man wears the usual scarf or diklo. Tapestry from the Welsh Folk Museum, St. Fagans, Cardiff.

After the etching of a Gypsy Fortune Teller by Caravaggio, 1573-1610. The young Caravaggio shocked the art world because he painted from nature, so there is no reason to doubt the authenticity of the Gypsy's dress - a turban, no longer in fashion, and the blanket worn over one shoulder. The original etching: Gabinetto Nazionale delle Stampe in Rome.

## IV  PROUD AS A PEACOCK

Due to their unquenchable spirit and inherent pride, the Gypsies were not prepared to integrate with gaujos to the extent of losing their own identity. They soon realized that their unusual and striking good looks could work for as well as against them, and they recognised the affinity between fear and awe. The fear of the people had adversely contributed to harsh legislation, while the awe in which they were held had been, and was to be a great advantage, particularly in their art of fortune telling.

From a 1611 woodcut illustrating one of the Italian Zingaresche poems, in vogue at the beginning of the C17. These describe the women's dress as 'head-dress with bands of cloth, a blanket wrapped round her and a gown all in the Gypsy style'.

The long journey to colder climes meant that some Gypsies were beginning to lose their tawny complexion. As usual their ingenuity stood them in good stead. Two seventeenth century tracts reveal how they enhanced their colour by various devices.

L'Abbé Prévost in his 'Contes, aventures et faits singuliers' (Tales, adventures and unusual occurrences) relates the bizarre sight presented to a traveller, on the bank of the Rhone. On a beach, he saw more than thirty naked men, lined up, exposed to and facing the sun. Naturally curious, he asked the cause of so interesting a ceremony. An elderly man replied that they were a harmless people known as Gypsies or Bohemiens, for whom it was necessary to be black or at least very tanned. And since nature did not entirely satisfy their needs, they employed a little artifice to supplement that which nature denied. He then showed some grease, which they rubbed on to help the action of the sun, and continued his explanation: The spot was more suitable than any other because having been browned by the sun during the day, in the evening they could go to some charcoal kilns close-by, where the smoke gave a longer lasting colour. The women were also there, but in the interest of modesty, they waited for the men to be reclothed before taking their place. The Gypsies assembled at the same spot every August, the month they found best for their purpose.

The Parisian doctor Charles Patin, in an account of a voyage in central Europe, published in 1673, relates another similar scene, on the edge of a meadow between the Elbe and a small wood: 'like an abridgement of the resurrection and the final judgement, three or four hundred people rose up from the ground where they had lain. They had not troubled to dress themselves, except for a few, who had jackets, but none had any embarrassment. It was company, or if you like a regiment of Bohemiens, not of those born in Bohemia, but Bohemiens by profession, who have no trade, no wealth, no friends, no industry, and who nevertheless existed with a freedom which you would not find in the most free republic in the world.'

Patin and his companions did not find any explanation for the phenomenon but there can be little doubt who these people were and what they were doing.

A notice about the Gypsies made in 1808 by an employee of the department of Mont-Tonnerre stated that while their colour was in general tawny, they often darkened themselves even more with an infusion of nut oil.

Heinrech Grellmann, in his Dissertation on the Gypsies, first published in Berlin in 1783, devoted a chapter to their dress. Despite his obvious relish in describing the poverty of the Gypsies he came into contact with, he fails to mask their pride in their appearance.

Grellmann thought that as their economy belonged to that of beggars, it was to be expected that they would exhibit poverty and described those first coming to Europe as ragged and miserable in appearance, excepting their leaders. He said that the men did not wear hats unless they wanted to make a figure, but even then, a rough cap was more usual. In winter, apart from Moldavia and Wallachia, where the women knitted socks, a couple of rags were wound round their feet; and as they didn't spin, sew or wash, their linen was no better, so their clothes were worn until they rotted and fell off. The men's dress often consisted of only a pair of breeches and a torn shirt.

However, Grellmann goes on to say 'We are not to suppose that the Gypsies dress so ill because they are indifferent about it, on the contrary, they love fine clothes to an extravagant degree: the want proceeds from necessity. Whenever an opportunity offers of acquiring a good coat, either by gift, purchase, or theft he immediately bestirs himself to become master of it, he puts it on directly, without attending, in the least, to whether it suits the rest of his apparel. If his dirty shirt had holes in it as big as a barn door, or his breeches were so out of condition that one might perceive their antiquity at the first glance; were he without shoes, stockings, or a hat, it would not prevent his strutting about in a laced coat, and valuing himself the more upon it, in case it happened to be a red one.  The Gypsies in Transilvania spend all their earnings in alehouses and on clothes.  Their dress is so particular, that it would excite laughter in the sternest philosopher, to see a Gypsy parading about, with a beaver hat, a silk or red cloth coat, at the same time his breeches torn, and his shoes or boots covered with patches.  They are particularly fond of clothes made after the Hungarian fashion, or which had been worn by peoples of distinction.'

To illustrate the similar situation in Hungary, Grellmann includes a passage from the Imperial Gazettes: 'Notwithstanding these people are so wretched, that they have nothing but rags to cover them, which do not fit at all, and are scarce sufficient to hide their nakedness; yet they betray their foolish taste and vain ostentation, whenever they have an opportunity.'

He tells us that while some of the Gypsies in Transilvania wear Wallachian dress, those in Hungary would rather go half naked, or wear a sack, than wear foreign clothes, however good.  They like green, but scarlet is preferred to all other colours.  For this reason, 'a man cannot appear abroad in a red habit, though worn out, without being surrounded by a crowd of Gypsies, old and young, who want to purchase from him, be it coat, pelisse, or breeches.  Unless severely pinched by the cold, or in case of the greatest necessity, they will not deign to put on a boors coat:  They rather chose to buy for their own use cast off clothes, if they happen to be ornamented with lace or loops, they strut about in such dresses, as proudly as if they were not only lords of the district, but of the whole creation.  Thus, they spend all the money they can spare, in such sort of clothes, as are not at all becoming their station, nor answer any other purpose, but to betray their silly notions, and expose them to the world.  They do not pay the least regard to symmetry, nor care what reasonable people think of their dress; if they can only get something shining to put on, that is eye-catching, they give themselves no concern whether the reft is very bad, or whether they have it not at all.  It is no uncommon spectacle to see a Gypsy parading the streets, in an embroidered pelisse, or laced coat trimmed with silver buttons, barefooted, hatless, and a dirty ragged shirt, or a pair of embroidered scarlet breeches, and perhaps no other covering but half a shirt.'

'Nothing pleases a Hungarian Gypsy so much as a pair of yellow (tschischmen) boots and spurs; no sooner do these glitter on his feet, but he bridles up, and marches consequentially about, often eying his fine boots, without minding that his breeches might be quite shabby.'

Of the women, Grellmann wrote that it was generally thought that they went beyond the men in filth and nastiness, and that their appearance was shocking to any civilized person. 'Their whole covering consisted of, either a piece of linen thrown over the head and wound round the thighs, or an old shift hung over them, through which the smoky hide appeared in numberless places. Sometimes in winter, they wrapped themselves in a piece of woollen stuff like a cloak. Occasionally they wore breeches or some other male clothing. Like the men they wore on their feet either a pair of knitted coarse socks common in Moldavia and Wallachia, or they bound them in rags, which remained until the stuff perished or fell off, or until the Spring, when both men and women went barefoot.

They are as fond of dress as the men, and equally ridiculous in it, often wearing a dress cap, while their rotten linen jacket, scarcely covers those parts which nature instructs us to conceal, or leave their smoked breasts open to view. In Spain they hang all sorts of trumpery in their ears, plaster their temples with great patches of black silk besides a number of baubles about the neck.'

The children, he tells us, ran naked until the age of ten, when the boys were given breeches and the girls aprons.

Grellmann concluded his dissertation by describing a custom adopted by the Gypsy men before a fight – a custom he considered laudable. The combatants would allow a truce to give time to strip to their shirts so that their clothes did not suffer in the fray. He pointed out that this was useful because anybody appearing in a ragged coat might affirm, on their honour, that it was not done in a Gypsy brawl.

Grellmann's words are a sharp reminder that in certain areas some Gypsies struggled to rise above poverty. Nonetheless, while, for practical reasons, they lived more simply – with less material clutter than gaujos, dress was every bit as, if not more important to them. They still strove to bolster their spirits with attractive clothing to their taste, and their tenacity usually led to success.

The children ran naked until the age of ten.

Abraham Wood

Abraham or Abram Wood FOUNDER OF THE CHIEF WELSH ROMANI CLAN WAS DESCRIBED BY HIS GREAT GRANDDAUGHTER SAIFORELLA WOOD was 'very tall but not so very lusty, and middling thin. His complexion was very dark, with rosy cheeks. His face was round as an apple and he had a double chin and a small mouth, very small for a man. He always rode on horseback, on a blood horse, and would not sleep in the open, but in barns. He wore a three·cocked hat with gold lace, a silk coat with swallow·tails – sometimes red, sometimes green, and sometimes black – and a waistcoat em-broidered with green leaves. The buttons on the coat were half·crowns, those on the waistcoat shillings. His breeches were white, tied with silk ribbons, and there were bunches of ribbons at the knees. On his feet he had pumps with silver buckles and silver spurs, and he wore two gold rings – only two – and a gold watch and chain.'

DORA YATES

# V CHAMELEONS OF THE 18th CENTURY

**B**y the eighteenth-century Gypsies were a familiar sight in the British Isles and the picturesque aspect of their lives continued to appeal to painters and poets - many of whom had a romantic vision. These artists missed the Gypsies' boldness and tough determination to survive, as well as their flamboyance, which enabled them to survive emotionally. In fact, these artists missed the very essence of the Gypsy character. This character and their way of life were revealed to a great extent by their stance and way of moving, like the saucy military walk of a great many of the men. Small details, which revealed the Gypsies' way of life were also missed. Details such as the thick cudgels, of about three feet in length, which the men carried, or the habit, when travelling, of wearing their breeches unbuttoned at the knees, and the heads of their socks rolled down leaving their knees bare and unencumbered.

The Gypsies of the eighteenth century were not just picturesque or shabby; they equalled their forebears in the glamour of their dress and the drama of their lives.

Abram Wood, who entered Wales in the early 1700s and became the father of the Welsh Gypsies, must have been a magnificent sight with his Gypsy looks and dressed in the finest fashion. Scotland too was able to boast a leader, who must have been equally striking. The head of the Ruthvens was a tall man, who when in full dress in his youth, wore a white wig, a ruffled shirt, a blue Scottish bonnet, scarlet breeches and waistcoat, blue superfine coat, white stockings and silver buckle shoes.

*Before, and long after, the year 1745, the male branches of the Baillies traversed Scotland, mounted on the best horses to be found in the country; themselves dressed in longcoats, made of the finest scarlet and green cloth, ruffled at hands & breast, booted and spurred; with cocked hats on their heads, pistols in their belts, and broad-swords by their sides: and at the heels of their horses followed greyhounds, and other dogs of the chase, for their amusement. Some of them assumed the manners and characters of gentlemen, which they supported with wonderful art and propriety. The females attended fairs in the attire of ladies, riding on ponies, with side saddles in the best style. Wilson's daughters were all frequently dressed in a very superior manner, & could not have been taken for Gypsies.*

A CHIEF, CHARLES WILSON
10 OFTEN DISPLAYED A GOLD
WATCH WITH MANY SEALS
ATTACHED TO ITS CHAIN, HAD
A FAMILY OF HANDSOME
DAUGHTERS

W SIMSON

From a painting by Thomas Gainsborough, 1727-1788. The Gypsies engraved by J. Wood, and published by J. Boydell 1764. The painting is also referred to as Wooded Landscape with Peasants indicating the confusion Gypsies caused. The clothes worn are by no means unique to Gypsies although the bodices are worn rather lower than usual, possibly because they lost their ruffled trims. According to Grellmann the baring of breasts was normal on the continent and may well have been in Britain.

Another Gypsy Chief, Charles Stewart, affirmed that he was descended from the royal Stuarts of Scotland – an assertion which his descendants maintained for a great many years and possibly to this day. In support of his claim, at a wedding in 1774, he wore a large cocked hat, decorated with a beautiful plume of white feathers, in imitation of the white cockade of the Pretender. On this occasion, he wore a short coat, philabeg (kilt) and purse, and tartan hose. Sometimes he wore a piece of brass like a star, on his left breast and he carried a cudgel.

Simson's great grandfather knew Gypsies such as these. He said that one of the Baillies was the handsomest, best dressed, best looking and the best bred man he ever saw. If this were not enough, he generally rode one of the best horses the kingdom could produce, 'himself attired in the finest scarlet, with his greyhounds following him as if he had been a man of the first rank'.

A great many of the men wore green coats, black breeches and leather aprons, and it was common to wear silver brooches on their breasts and gold rings on their fingers, or gold watches, sometimes with seals attached to the chains.

The women were as fashionable as the men and frequently dressed in a superior manner. They attended the fairs in ladies' attire, riding ponies side-saddle, in the best of style, and they were partial to green clothes.

The natural ease and the confidence of the Gypsies combined with their fashionable dress enabled them to pass themselves off as gentlefolk, when the need arose. Had they indulged in some of their taste for gold or silver ornament, they would have at once become recognisable.

These wonderful clothes were equalled by a flair for dramatic, daring, even shocking behaviour.

It was common practice for old female Gypsies of authority to strip, without hesitation, defenceless individuals of their clothing, when they met them in secluded places. On one occasion Mary Yorkston happened to meet a shepherd's wife in the wild hills of Stobo and stripped her of all her clothes. The shepherd was horrified to see his wife approaching home without a stitch on!

Another shepherd came across Jean Gordon stripping a woman of her clothing. He at once assisted the helpless victim at which Jean drew from below her garments a dagger and threw it at him. Evading the blow, the shepherd closed in and striking her over the head with his staff, knocked her to the ground.

Taking it into account that the Gypsies, in their native country, would not have worn a great deal but often went about in a state little short of nudity, the extreme indecency of the following singular incident is somewhat lessened. The inhabitants of Winchburgh and neighbourhood were one day astonished to see a woman, with a child in her arms, walking along the road, as naked as when she was born. She told the country people that she had just been plundered and stripped of every piece of her clothing by a band of Tinkers, to whom she pointed, lying in a field close by. She submitted her piteous condition to the humanity of the inhabit-ants, begging for any sort of garment to cover her nakedness. The state in which she was found left not the slightest doubt on the minds of the spectators as to the truth of her predicament. Almost every female in the neighbourhood found some piece of clothing for the unfortunate woman; so that in a short time, she was not only comfortably clad, but had many articles of dress to spare. Shortly after she left the town homeward bound. But someone, observing the incident more closely than the rest, was astounded to see her go straight to the very Tinkers who she said were the culprits. Her appearance among her band convulsed them all with laughter at the dexterous trick she had played upon the simple inhabitants.

Esther Grant was another old-fashioned Gypsy celebrated for the practice of stripping people of their clothing. The Arabian principle on meeting a stranger in the desert expressed in the words 'Undress thyself – my wife is in want of a garment' suited the inclination of Gypsy women.

The ingenuity of the Gypsies knew no bounds. The women wore on their forefingers, rings of a peculiar construction, yet not appearing unusual, except for their very large size. On closing the hand, pressure was put on a spring, which in turn shot a sharp piece of steel through an aperture in the ring, like a bee thrusts and withdraws its sting. With these cute instruments, the Gypsy women were able to cut the pockets of their unsuspecting victims.

It is as well to remember that at the time the majority of the gaujos were still hostile to Gypsies and furthermore, many gaujos would commit crimes and defraud their own people without compunction. It is also as well to remember that where the Gypsies found friendship, they showed loyalty.

The greater part of the tenantry were kind to the Gypsies encouraging them to visit their premises, and it was not unknown for gaujos to participate in entertainments or meals provided by the principal Gypsies. There was great strength of attachment felt by the Gypsies for such people, and when some of the landed proprietors introduced clauses in their leases prohibiting their tenants from harbouring them, they naturally expressed great indignation.

In general, the Gypsies still thought it was morally acceptable to defraud gaujos to whom they were under no obligation.

To suit their deceptions both the men and women often changed their clothing as many as four or five times in one fair day. Simson tells how McDonald and Jamieson often dressed elegantly in the finest and most fashionable clothes, with linen to correspond. At the same time they were perfect chameleons respecting their appearance and apparel. McDonald was frequently observed in three or four different outfits in one market-day. At one time of day he assumed the appearance and manners of a highland gentleman in full costume, completely attired in the best tartan. At another time, he appeared on horseback, ruffled at his hands and breast, booted and spurred, as if he were a man of some consideration. And then again, he would be seen in a ragged coat, with a budget and wallet on his back – a common travelling Tinker.

Simson's father, when a young lad, saw a large band of ragged and miserable Gypsies taking up their quarters in an old outhouse on a farm occupied by his family. Next morning, he went to see them decamp and saw among other articles of luggage, a large and heavy sack put on one of the asses. As the Gypsies were fastening it to the animal's back, it burst open and most of the contents tumbled out. Among these he was surprised to see a great many excellent cocked hats, suits of fine green cloths, greatcoats and several handsome saddles and bridles. By strange expressions and odd manoeuvres, they endeavoured to drive him away and divert his attention from this singular sight, which revealed their clever practice. This practice of carrying with them superior clothing, so unlike their ordinary wretched wear, enabled the ingenious Gypsies to disguise themselves whenever the need arose.

The following anecdote also illustrates the 'gallant guise' in which these wanderers at one time rode through Scotland.

About the year 1768, early in the morning of the Peebles fair, two gentlemen were seen riding along the only road leading to Simson's

These illustrations are adapted from George Morland, 1763-1804. The first is from Gypsies in a Landscape c.1790, Bristol Museum and Art Gallery. The second is from The Gypsies' Tent. An engraving from the original was published by B. B. Evans, April 1793.

George Morland painted direct representations without sentimentality. He knew his subjects well and enjoyed the company of Gypsies. There is no reason whatever to doubt the authenticity of their dress in his depictions.

grandfather's farm. One of the servants was immediately told to put the parlour in order to receive the strangers, as, from their respectable appearance, seen at a distance, it was supposed they were friends coming to breakfast, before going to the market; a custom common enough in the country. However, the preparation proved unnecessary as the strangers rode rapidly past the house and dismounted at the door of an old nearly roofless sheep smearing-house, some three hundred yards further on. As they passed, it was observed that they were neatly dressed in long green coats, cocked hats, spurred riding boots, armed with broad-swords, and mounted on handsome grey horses, saddled and bridled; in short, everything in style and of the best quality. The people about the farm were extremely curious to know the identity of these handsomely turned out gentlemen, who stopped at this wretched hovel, where a band of Tinkers were quartered. Soon curiosity was satisfied and much mirth excited, when the gallant horsemen proved to be none other than James and William Baillie, sons of old Matthew Baillie, who, with part of his tribe was in the old house, making horn spoons. But the farm people were even more surprised, when, immediately afterwards, some of the Gypsy women set out for the fair, wearing very superior dresses, with the air of ladies in the middle ranks of society. The women of this tribe also rode to the fairs at Moffat and Beggar, very gaily dressed, with their ponies side-saddled and bridled. The men wore scarlet cloaks reaching their knees, resembling the Spanish fashion of the time

This love of extravagant fashion and ingenious stratagems went hand in hand with loyalty to ancient traditions.

We know from John Sampson, who had an extraordinary knack for uncovering esoteric material about Gypsies and the first person to learn the fluent inflected Romani, spoken in Wales, that at least some Gypsies retained the ancient custom of plaiting their hair throughout the eighteenth century, continuing into the twentieth. Another, more primitive custom, the virginal girdle survived well into the nineteenth century, when its use fell away because the strength of Gypsy culture, which fiercely protected women's virginity until marriage made it redundant. These customs illustrate the deep innate conservatism, as well as the morality of the Gypsy people at that time.

The Blewetts 'were the most swarthy and barbarous looking people I ever saw...

This Gypsy potter was a thick-set, stout man, above the middle size. He was dressed in an old dark-blue frock coat, with a profusion of black, greasy hair, which covered the upper part of his broad shoulders. He wore a high crowned, narrow-brimmed, old hat, with a lock of his black hair hanging down before each ear, in the same manner as the Spanish Gypsies are described by Swinburn. He also wore a pair of old full-topped boots, pressed half-way down his legs, and wrinkled about his ankles, like buskins. His visage was remarkably dark and gloomy. He walked up & down the market alone, without speaking to anyone, with a peculiar air of independence about him, as he twirled in his hand, in the Gypsy manner, by way of amusement, a strong bludgeon, about three feet long, which he held by the centre.

The females wore black Gypsy bonnets. The visage of the eldest one was remarkably long, her chin resting on her breast. These three old Gypsies were altogether, so dark, grim and outlandish looking, that they had little or no appearance of being natives of Britain.'

The Blewetts

The Gypsies also might be seen
On some occasions very clean,
Their younger women did delight
At feast times to be dressed in white
And with a ribbon round the waist
Of colour as might suit the taste;
The fastening behind you know
Was hid beneath a monstrous bow
While lace and jewels might bedeck
The breast, the bosom, and the neck;
Nor could the country girls surpass
The dress worn by the Gypsy lass.
Also at feasts, in summertime,
The men would dress up in their prime:

Large silver buckles very bright
They had to keep their shoes on tight,
And clean white stockings they displayed
How handsomely the leg was made;
Their breeches, buttoned at the knees,
Were made so as to fit with ease,
And just below you might see half
A broad red garter round each calf;
Sometimes they wore a nice red vest
With silver buttons down the breast;
A long black coat of velveteen,
With silver buttons bright and clean,
The coat as soft as any down,
The buttons big as half a crown
What I have here described with care
The jovial Gypsies used to wear.

FROM GYPSIES OF
NORTHAMPTONSHIRE
DAVID TOWNSEND

The Gypsies of Northamptonshire, published 1877 Kettering:
David Townsend's verse account of Gypsies circa 1830

# VI  THE GOLDEN AGE

## Nineteenth Century

Murray, a Scottish Tinker, painted a fascinating picture of Gypsy dress in the first half of the nineteenth century, from which some parallels may be drawn with earlier dress on the continent.

He said the old men wore knee breeches, which they made themselves from cashmere, when buck or sheepskin was unobtainable, and also leggings, which buttoned at the back. They wore two waistcoats (baiengri), the outer one sleeved and of plush, with two rows of pearl buttons down the front and three buttons on each pocket flap. A Gypsy, Julius Caesar, had silver buttons to his inside coat and two rows of gold pieces – a favourite decoration with the old Gypsies – to button down the outer. Their boots had tongues, which hung out, and very short rounded toe-caps, with four rows of nails with palantines in the top. And to top this, round the neck they wore watch-guards (roringeras), made from coral beads, from which hung great watches with close on half a pound of silver in the case. Stunning as they must have been, they were of little practical use since few could tell the time.

They carried knitted horse-hair purses about ten inches (25.4cm) long with beads at each end worked into about six stars and a half moon. A slit up the middle divided the purse into a side for gold and another for silver, and to close they were screwed up with bone rings, which they carved themselves.

Occasionally the Gypsies dyed their clothes - the old men particularly favouring yellow waistcoats and green coats.

The old men wore cloaks made from skins riveted together with fine little nails made of copper pieces or old card pennies. They were tied by a knot on each shoulder, giving a curious appearance, and some of them, for grandeur, were worn brought together like a bunch of ribbons on one shoulder, with copper hooks in front. While the latter were almost certainly survivals of the toga, all these cloaks would appear to be survivals and variations of the fleece or goat skin kaunakes of the Sumerian civilization, which continued in this form or as a cloth imitating skins, until well into the Middle Ages.

Lambs were also killed and their skins put by for winter when lambskin (brokla's burk) shirts were worn, while in summer they wore calico.

The oldest wore their hair in three plaits, one down the back and two tails either side, while on their faces they wore moustaches with narrow whiskers coming right down each side, leaving their chins clean shaven. The younger generation wore black curls falling each side, with a crooked parting in the front.

The Gypsy men always had a white hat with small brought-up-sloped crown and broad leaf, which they would travel fifty miles for. They wore earrings made of copper and rings on both hands, one on the little finger and three on each of the others. Some had bracelets on the wrist and old Golias Gezias, the oldest man of the generation, wore them on his ankles and to the grave as well.

In the winter they wore 'bizemblis' round their necks. These were made from rabbit skins or other fur, and lined with silk, similar to those worn by ladies when walking out. Later some took to wearing posnakos or grinders (kerchiefs), doubtless the forerunners to the diklo.

Clothes were so important to Gypsies that they were not always burnt at death but kept in chests, which passed from generation to generation for up to three hundred years. Sam Fiansi who was close on eighty-six years, showed one to Murray containing his great grandfather's clothes, and he raved like a child when he thought of the old people and the old days. He claimed that he had refused a hundred and twenty bars of gold for this chest, which was more than three hundred years old. Murray gave Sampson this description around 1890 so the chest would seem to date back to before 1590. How common this custom was is uncertain, but it rather defies the notion that the Gypsies' clothes were always burnt after death.

During this period the women's dress was a typical amalgamation of the past, their idiosyncratic likes, and the fashion of the time. Their dresses were short bodiced, buttoned up close round the neck, with the tops of two rams' horns for buttons in the middle of the back; the sleeves reached just above the elbows, and the skirts hung down straight to near the ankles. The fabric was striped - one baro yuk (big stripe) and one bitti yuk (little stripe). The short bodice had been introduced into fashion in the late eighteenth century, continuing until the 1830s, and narrow stripes amongst other simple patterns were fashionable, so the Gypsy women had typically adopted and adapted fashion to their own sense of style. They wore small shoes with big buckles, made by the men and which they polished up every morning with brick dust.

Their gads (shirts) were made of calf skin for winter, and gauze or very fine cloth in summer, coloured by themselves – sometimes yellow. Like the men, they made use of their knowledge of natural dyes. Their winter petticoats were also of skin – goat or sheep, with the hair on, and harder to imagine, their stockings were the same, some with button fastenings.

They wore red and grey cloaks reaching to the heels, which had hoods with draw-strings, and they would go miles to find a particular grey wool for their making. However, red cloaks, which they often dyed themselves, were the most common.

Their hats were like the old Welsh hats, brought up very small and tall, such as the ones associated with witches. Sometimes they wore bands of fine cloth wrapped around and around their head and decorated with rosettes – one each side at the front and three at the back. And more too, you'd see an old woman with as many stars on her head as there are in the sky. And as many rings, beads and earrings as they could carry on them; and the bigger they were, the better they were pleased! Some of their rings and bracelets were very old and Murray instanced some that the Lees had that were nearly three hundred years old which would date them back to the late sixteenth century. As for the bands of cloth or turbans, and the wealth of jewellery worn, these are but more reminders of their origins.

An even more interesting survival, although not exactly part of their dress, was the virginal girdle worn by the young Gypsy girls as a safeguard of purity before marriage. This was a six-inch band of pure wool on a very light skin – usually eel (snig) skin, which had been tanned and dried for a good number of days, and then steamed to the right thickness. It was worn between the legs and tied up on the back – being put on in the morning and removed at night by the mother. The fine wool on the inside and the cured skin enabled the wearer to urinate and no more. They were worn from about the age of twelve until marriage, when it was carried before the bride in a baro kosht (wooden boat), so that her rom (husband) knew that she was good. After the wedding it was put in a box for her daughter and one might pass several generations for 'hundreds and hundreds of years', although one hopes this was the exception rather than the rule.

An article of 1856 on the Gypsies of Egypt states that until marriage the young female Fehemis wore a cincture of silk or cotton thread round the loins in token of virginity, and that among the Helebis the dilk (zone of chastity) was often made of plaited leather, and cut off on the wedding night. In the case of the Kurbats, they wore a cloth constantly until marriage, when the husband alone was allowed to take it off.

In The Zincali, 1841, Borrow points to the 'dicle.' He says, 'Reasons, which may easily be judged, render it impossible for us to be very explicit on this point, it will be permitted to us, however, to state that no females in the world wear their interior drapery in the same manner as the Gitanas, and this drapery or dicle of the female children is invariably fastened by their mothers, after a peculiar and singular fashion, and is never removed, but continually inspected by the latter until the day previous to marriage.' And in a description of a Gypsy marriage he refers to the mysterious dicle, and yet more mysterious handkerchief of cambric – the latter unspotted – for otherwise there would have been no wedding. This tells us that at least some of the girls wore a fabric next to their body and did not have to put up with wool.

Another custom, which for a time continued into the nineteenth century was that of changing their clothing to avoid detection. Simson told how, around 1820, Alexander Brown and his brother-in-law Wilson, who, like many of their race, were very handsome, like their forebears not only assumed the clothing of gentlemen but also the manners, which they imitated to a wonderful degree. When in full dress, Brown wore a highly ornamented hat trimmed with beautiful gold lace, which was then fashionable among the first rank in Scotland, particularly among army officers. His long-tailed coat was made of green superfine cloth and had one row of buttons at the breast. His shirt was the finest quality, ruffled at hands and breast and worn with a buckled black stock round the neck. He also wore on his handsome boots, silver-plated spurs – all in the fashion of the day. Below his clothing he carried a large knife and, in the shaft or butt-end of his large whip, a small spear or dagger was concealed. Wilson often dressed in a similar way and both rode the best horses in the country.

When away on business, Brown presented the appearance of a smart English merchant traveller on horseback, but on his way home at some isolated spot the 'equestrian Tinker' would disrobe, pack up his finery and then assume his ragged coat, leathern apron and budget, before venturing among his people. Here was an instance of a haughty overbearing man wearing the best of clothing and mounted on the best of steeds, metamorphosed in an instant into a poor wandering, beggarly and pitiful Gypsy.

Although some Gypsies continued the practice of changing their appearance, increasingly this custom was abandoned. Several factors were responsible. The repeal in 1780 of the severe legislation against them, combined with their increasing prosperity and acceptance by the rest of society meant that now, when Gypsies changed their clothes, it was for work, some occasion or a celebration. The increasing security led to the whalebone whip replacing the cudgel or knife as the symbol of the male Gypsies' strength, while the knife was concealed and kept for practical use only and not for display.

Dramatic contrasts were still a feature of Gypsy dress, but now the differences were between families and individuals.

Borrow painted a picture of the Gypsies becoming part of the countryside. 'In no part of the world is the Gypsy life more in accordance with the general idea that the Gypsy is like Cain – a wanderer on the face of the earthy – than in England; for there, the covered cart and the little tent are the houses of the Gypsy, and he seldom remains more than three days in the same place. So conducive is the climate of England to beauty, that nowhere else is the appearance of the race so prepossessing as in that country. Their complexion is dark, but not disagreeably so; their faces are oval, their features regular, their foreheads rather low, and their hands and feet small. The men are taller than the English peasantry, and far more active. They all speak the English language with fluency, and in their gait and demeanour are easy and graceful; in both respects standing in striking contrast with the peasantry, who, in speech, are slow and uncouth, and in manner, dogged and brutal.'

Richard and William Howitt also saw the Gypsies as part of Rural England, despite their easily distinguishable looks – their jet black hair, black sparkling eyes, Indian complexions and oriental language. Silvanus Lovell, a Gypsy himself, evoked a similar idyllic scene of the same period, circa 1830.

'Why you'd see the lanes then crowded with Romane – Lovells and Boswells and Stanleys and Hernes and Chilcotts. Something like Gypsies they were, with their riding horses, real hunters to ride to the fairs and wakes on, and the women with their red cloaks and high old-fashioned beaver hats, and the men in beautiful silk velvet coats and white and yellow satin waistcoats, and all on 'em booted and spurred.'

As in the previous century the Gypsies' choice of clothes was by no means unique to them, but as before they were particular to satisfy their taste - a taste that admirably suited their distinctive looks. There was nothing anaemic about this guise, nor about the Gypsies themselves. Tartans, striped or check cloths; brightly coloured shawls or handkerchiefs, which were sometimes worn under their black beaver bonnets, together with the red cloaks; all complemented their physical characteristics as well as their spirits.

They are not to be confounded with a tribe of wandering potters, who live in tents like them. The true
Gypsies are readily distinguished by their invariable jet-black hair, black sparkling eyes, Indian
complexions, and their genuine oriental language.
The women, many of them, in their youth, are fine
strapping figures, with handsome brown faces and
most brilliant and speaking eyes, · they have a peculiar poco-curante air and jaunty gait, and are extremely fond of finery. Their costume is unique and
pretty uniform, · scarlet cloaks, black beaver hats
with broad slouching brims, or black velvet bonnets
with large wide pokes trimmed with lace; a handkerchief thrown over the head under the bonnet, and
tied beneath the chin; long pendant ear-rings,
black stockings, and ankle-boots.

WILLIAM HOWITT

William Howitt, 1792-1879   The Rural Life of England 1838

The Gypsies were increasingly held in awe on account of their fortune-telling, powers of healing and mastery of curses.   They continued to become acquainted with the gentry and well-to-do and from these sources often acquired their clothes.   It was no longer necessary to resort to the drastic measures of the previous centuries.  Betsy Wood, a descendant of Abram (Wood) gave an example.

Betsy and Syforella were out calling and visited a cottage, where a sick woman lay.   The invalid pleaded with Syforella, saying that she would give all she possessed for a cure since all other remedies had failed.   The Gypsy seeing a red and black flowered silk gown, hanging by the fire, asked for it, causing another woman to step forward and claim that it was hers brought out in readiness for a wedding.  A wrangle followed until a man came and joined in, ending the dispute by giving

Syforella the dress. The two Gypsies then turned to go, leaving a frantic invalid pleading for her cure. 'I have promised, all will be performed. I will come to thee in the morning.'

Next day the Gypsy returned with a bottle of water from the well at Glan-y-Mor. She bathed the patient with the water and bound cloths, dipped in it, around her head, saying that it was blessed water with the power to break curses. The Gypsy administered the water several times and before leaving the neighbourhood the promised cure was complete.

The Gypsy women also had their clothes made by able seamstresses, enabling them to have their grey silk spencers and smart flowered chintz petticoats, as well as their outer wear to be a perfect fit and quality. The best hatters and milliners also received their custom.

But not all were able to afford this kind of luxury, so contrasts in their appearance were still part of their life. Borrow saw and recorded these extremes. 'I was not, however, without apprehension, which indeed, the appearance of these two people was well calculated to inspire. The woman was a stout figure, seemingly between thirty and forty; she wore no cap, and her long hair fell on either side of her head, like horse-tails, half way down to her waist; her skin was dark and swarthy, like that of a toad, and the expression of her countenance was particularly evil; her arms were bare, and her bosom was but half-concealed by a slight bodice, below which she wore a coarse petticoat, her only other article of dress. The man was somewhat younger, but of a figure equally wild; his frame was long and lathy, but his arms were remarkably short, his neck was rather bent, he squinted slightly, and his mouth was much awry; his complexion was dark, but, unlike that of the woman, was more ruddy than livid; there was a deep scar on his cheek, something like the impression of a halfpenny. The dress was quite in keeping with the figure; in his hat, which was slightly peaked, was stuck a peacock's feather, over a waistcoat of hide, untanned and with the hair upon it, he wore a rough jerkin of russet hue; small clothes of leather, which had probably once belonged to a soldier, but with which pipe-clay did not seem to have come in contact for many a year, protected his lower man as far as the knee; his legs were cased in long stockings of blue worsted, and on his shoes he wore immense old fashioned buckles. Such were the two beings who now came rushing upon me.'

What a difference from their son Mr Petulengro and his wife, who visited Borrow in the dingle. He was dressed in Roman fashion in a smartly cut sporting coat, with half-crown buttons; a scarlet and black waistcoat with spaded half-guinea buttons over a fine white Holland shirt.  His breeches were velveteen-corduroy, the cords exceedingly broad; he had buff cloth leggings, furred at the bottom and on his feet were highlows.  He wore a high-peaked hat, similar to the Spanish 'calane', favoured by the bravos of Seville and Madrid.  Mrs Petulengro was also dressed in Roman fashion.  Her lustrous black hair fell in braids on either side of her head.  She wore earrings with long drops of gold, and her necklace was of very large pearls, somewhat tarnished, and apparently of considerable antiquity.

Another striking figure was Gilderoy Scamp (1812-1893), king of the Kentish Gypsies.  A tall dark man, with a wrinkled face and piercing eyes, he usually wore a black frockcoat, white knee-breeches and a white beaver hat stuck rakishly on one side, over his unkempt locks.  According to local tradition, Scamp's hats were given to him by the late Baron Mayer de Rothschild in return for his vote in a Hythe parliamentary election.

The Gypsies connections with Royalty and the aristocracy continued as did their own hierarchical tradition.

The Faas of Jedbergh, in Northumberland, were a close-knit and largely non-nomadic community.  The Royalty of this singular group had their own ceremonial robes, which, partly due to their isolation did not reflect the dress of other Gypsy Royals.

Will Faa recalled a Royal event when Queen Victoria visited Dunbar and the Gypsies.  On this occasion the Gypsy Queen, her mother-in-law and her sister-in-law were dressed in purple and velvet and the men wore scarlet coats.

Queen Victoria and the Gypsies shared a mutual high regard. A note from the Queen's diary, August 1878, describes another visit with the Royal party to Knockindale Hill: "where were stationed in best attire the Queen of the Gypsies, an oldish woman with yellow handkerchief on her head and a youngish very dark and truly Gypsy-like woman in velvet and a red shawl. The Queen is a thorough Gypsy, with a scarlet cloak and a yellow handkerchief around her head. Men in red hunting coats, all very dark and all standing on a platform, bowed and waved their handkerchiefs."

Queen Victoria was held in warm affection by her Gypsy subjects and this warmth remained undiminished towards all her successors.

King Edward VII, when Prince of Wales, often tossed a gold sovereign to the famous Matty Cooper. Known as the 'Windsor Froggie,' Matty usually wore typical Roman rig – a yellow and red neckerchief, knee breeches and black cut-away coat.

Athaliah Shaw was about the ugliest Romani I ever saw, standing close on six feet high, with a face like a vicious horse, and hair as coarse as his tail. She wore a long bright tartan shawl, draped awry, an old black straw bonnet on her head, with a green and yellow handkerchief under it, a rusty black dress, and boots like a navigator's. Uncle Euri, who came lounging up a few hundred yards behind her, with a couple of terriers at his heels, was a thickset, sturdy fellow, of six-and-forty,

GROOME DESCRIBES THE EXCEPTIONS TO THE IDEAL OF GYPSY LOOKS AS WELL AS THOSE FULFILLING IT

brown as a hazel-nut, with small black eyes, a coloured handkerchief loosely twisted round his
bronzed throat, a fur cap on his head, a long calf-
skin sleeved waistcoat, loose drab breeches, 2 leggings
half unbuttoned over his strong ankle-boots.

A hale old man, he stands over six foot-    SILVANUS LOVELL
two; his merry nutbrown face is lighted up by dazzling teeth and a pair of glittering hazel eyes; his
grizzling hair curls round the brim of a highcrown-
ed ribbon-decked hat. A yellow silk neckerchief, brown
velveteen coat with crown-piece buttons, red waistcoat with spade-guinea dittos, cord breeches, and
leathern leggings, make up his holiday attire; his
left hand wields a silver-headed whalebone whip; and
from a deep skirt-pocket peeps forth the unfailing
violin.      Straight, lithe, and able to    LEMENTINA LOVELL
walk three miles an hour, handsome    IS NOT MUCH LIKE A
                                      GRANDMOTHER BUT
withal, if somewhat weatherworn. In    THEN SHE IS ONLY
                                      FIFTY SEVEN YEARS
girlhood she is said to have strongly resembled her beautiful kinswoman Charlotta Stanley,
and still she retains her girlhood's ornaments. A
gorgeous handkerchief covers her coalblack curiously
plaited hair; her ears are pierced by old-fashioned
hoops of heavy gold; a necklace of amber, coral 2 coins
runs thrice about her neck; and her hands are bed-
izened with massy rings, one of them wrought by

Plato from a guinea welded upon three wedding rings. A parti-coloured apron over a short blue woollen dress, 2 naily boots, AND A CUTTY PIPE COMPLETE HER 'LANDSCAPE'

Francis Hindes Groome, In Gipsy Tents, 1880

Simson tells us of perhaps the most extraordinary dress worn by Gypsies in the nineteenth century. Near Inverkeithing, he once saw twelve young girls, travelling on a cart drawn by a shaggy pony. They were all neatly attired, but most notable were those in trousers with frills about the ankles, who, according to Simson, few would have taken for Gypsies.

As this was fifty years ahead of the time when trousers would have been worn, the question remains, were they wearing frilled drawers or bloomers? At this time, these had been introduced from America, but they did not become generally popular being considered immodest and unladylike. The Gypsies would not have shared these scruples. Such typical independence in dress was carried over to formal occasions like funerals and weddings, and into the twentieth century.

At the wedding of Rosaina to Harry Locke, the bride was resplendent in a red silk frock; and adorned with several gold bangles and finger-rings, while the groom wore a new suit of green velveteen and a hat decorated with peacock's feathers.

And the Edinburgh Evening Dispatch of August 20th, 1890 reported the marriage between Owen Smith of Reading and Ellen Lee of Brighton, which was officiated by the Reverend Arthur Robbin, Chaplain to the Queen and the Prince of Wales. 'The bride's costume was a terra-cotta gown, tied with a broad satin sash, and she wore a wreath of orange blossoms and white tulle veil, and carried a handsome bouquet. The bridesmaids' costumes were similar to that of the bride with the exception of the head-dresses, which consisted of large straw hats, trimmed with white ostrich feathers and ribands.'

The custom of wearing white for weddings, which began in the mid-eighteenth century was still not fully established country wide. As usual the Gypsies lagged behind current trends taking their time to cast aside their traditional bright colours. It was not until the twentieth century that they began to conform and wear white for weddings and black for funerals.

The predominant colours of the nineteenth century, as in the eighteenth, were yellow, green and red. Block said that yellow was the colour of suffering, without any further explanation. Obviously, Gypsies have suffered, but it is far more likely that the love of yellow is simply due to the brightness of the colour and its resemblance to gold. It is the wearing of gay colours and the display of opulence that has helped them to overcome hardship and the emotions it engenders.

The Sinti used to think very highly of the colour green, they loved green borders on their clothes and green collars on their coats. If a Sinto was 'Prastapen,' i.e., excluded from his tribe, he was forbidden to wear green clothes.

The red cloaks, so highly favoured by the Gypsy women in the nineteenth century, were probably in the early years a russet hue, as shown in William Shayer's paintings; but there can be no doubt that as soon as bright red cloths were available, the more sombre tones would have been abandoned.

Although red cloaks and green coats were not worn exclusively by the Gypsies, they must have looked especially striking on them, in part because the men enlivened their coats, giving them an air of opulence, by the addition of gold and silver buttons – Ryley Boswell's were golden guineas.

When Julia Lee (née Boswell) wore her long white fur-lined, red cloak, which she wore into the twentieth century, she must have looked just as opulent as Ryley and even more striking, arousing the same sort of awe as Vivien Lee in the leading role of Gone with the Wind, or a film star does today in a top designer or couturier's outfit. Under her cloak she always wore a black satin blouse with beads on it, and white stone diaper pinnies, which she made herself.

Most Gypsy characteristics were carried into the twentieth century, including the pocket and apron.

Betsy Wood wore a Holland cloth apron, which she made and trimmed with two little heart-shaped pockets, fancifully edged with red braid, to hold her money and other small articles. Beneath the apron, Betsy wore a larger pocket, where she kept a screw of tobacco and her little black pipe. She also wore a coral necklace and wrapped herself in a red Paisley shawl.

This is typical dress of the first part of the twentieth century. The pocket, which was usually embroidered and worn under the apron was adopted from the gaujos, but like so many other adopted forms of dress, its practicality meant it was used by the Gypsies for a far longer period. As these separate pockets were abandoned, those on the aprons or 'pinnas' assumed the same characteristics – being large and fancy.

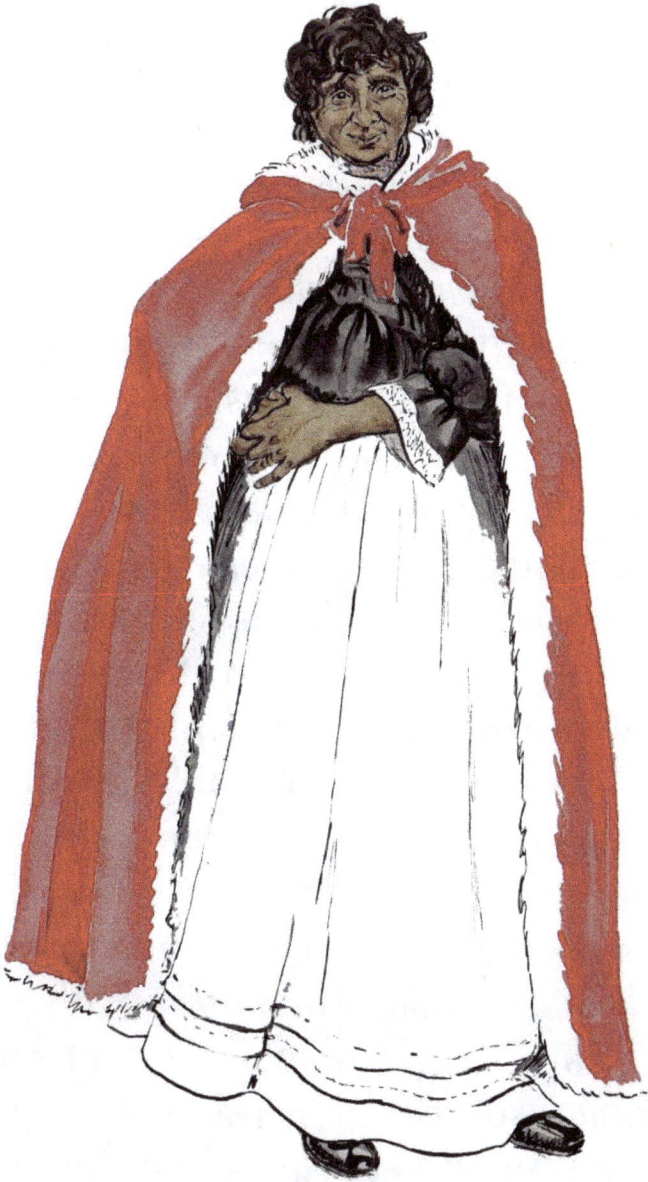

Julia Lee (née Boswell)

Mary Yorkston was fully six feet in stature, stout made in her pers-

on, with very strongly marked and harsh features; and had, altogether, a very imposing aspect and manner. She wore a large black beaver hat, tied down over her ears with a handkerchief, knotted below her chin, in the Gypsy fashion. Her upper garment was a dark-blue short cloak, somewhat after the Spanish fashion, made of substantial woollen cloth, approaching to superfine in quality. The greater part of her other apparel was made of dark-blue camlet cloth with petticoats so short that they scarcely reached to the calves of her well-set legs. (Indeed, all the females among the Baillies wore petticoats of the same length). Her stockings were of dark-blue worsted, flowered & ornamented at the ankles with scarlet thread; & in her shoes she displayed large, massy, silver buckles. The whole of her habiliments were very substantial, with not a rag or rent to be seen about her person. (She was sometimes dressed in a green gown, trimmed with red ribbons.) Her outer petticoat was folded up round her haunches, for a lap, with a large pocket dangling at each side; and below her cloak she carried, between her shoulders, a small flat pack, or pad, which contained her most valuable articles. About her person she generally kept a large clasp-knife, with a long, broad blade, resembling a dagger or carving-knife; and carried in her hand a long pole or pike-staff, that reached about a foot above her head.

A History of the Gypsies, published 1865, but written twenty years or more earlier
by Walter Simson

The nineteenth century saw Gypsies using less radical means to obtain their clothes - some learning to sew and make their own. Betsy Wood not only made her aprons, but made and embroidered a smock, as well as a black and white, steel buttoned shirt for her lucky husband. When sharing quarters in a barn with Blind Ellen, Betsy used to brush and tidy a corner, where they would work together. The old lady, who cut and made her dresses wonderfully well by sense of touch, sat cross-legged with Betsy squatting beside her, hemming the many flounces to adorn the skirt of a new dress. The old woman would say, "The feel of the silk is good. Thou art sure, girl, that the colour is pretty? I would not be clad in gloom." And Betsy assured her that it was bright and cheerful, being a predominately red tartan.

During the period 1904-5, a Gypsy friend would invite Dora Yates into her shining clean van, and produce some fine lace edging she had made for her 'crumb-cloths', or a frock she had made that was exquisitely stitched together.

And a Gypsy folk tale tells us that the art of needlework had been acquired early in the nineteenth century. According to the tale: 'One day Happy Boz'll took his dog hunting. Two hares started up, but the dog couldn't run after both of them at once. However, just then, the dog ran against a scythe-blade cutting itself in two. One half of the dog ran after one hare and caught it, while the other half ran after the second hare and caught it. The hares were brought to Happy's feet. Then the two halves of the dog came together again, and the dog died. Happy took off the skin and used it to patch his knee-breeches. Just a year afterwards, to the very day, his breeches burst open and barked at him.'

*Now come in groups the Gypsy tribes,*
*From northern hills, from southern plains;*
*And many a panniered ass is swinging*
*The child that to itself is singing*
*Along the flowery lanes.*

Stout men are loud in wrangling talk,
  Where older tongues are gruff and tame;
  Keen maiden laughter rings aloft,
  Whilst many an undervoice is soft
  From many a talking dame.

  Their beaver hats are weather stained,-
  The one black plume is sadly gay;
  Their squalid brats are slung behind,
  In cloaks that flutter to the wind,
  Of scarlet, brown, and grey.

The slouching hat our hero wore,
  The crown wherewith he king was crowned;
  Wherein a pipe and crow's feather
  Were stuck in fellowship together,
  Was by a hundred winters browned.

His sceptre was a stout oak sapling,
  Round which a snake well carved was wreathed;
  Cunning and strength that well bespoke,
  Whilst from his frame, as from an oak,
  · Deliberate valour breathed ·

His footstool was the solid earth;
  His court spread out in pomp before him,
  The heath arrayed in summer smiles;
  His empire broad the British isles;
  His dome the heavens arched o'er him.

Antique and flowing was his dress;
And from his temples bold and bare,
Fell back in many a dusky tress,
As liberal as the wilderness,
His ample growth of hair.

GYPSY KING
RICHARD HOWITT

Like Cromwell's was his hardy front,
Where thought but feeling none was shown;
Where underneath a flitting grace,
Was firmly built up in his face,
A hardness as of stone.

Solomon was dressed in corduroys, with a wide brimmed Spanish brig-and's hat and a brilliant waistcoat tightly laced at the back, and the old woman (Sarah) in a black velvet bodice with scarlet sleeves and a short scarlet plaid skirt, which displayed her bare brown legs up to the knees.

My Gypsy Days, Dora Yates

# VII  THE AFTER GLOW

## Twentieth Century

Black-eyed Abigail Smith ranked high as a Fortune Teller in both the nineteenth and twentieth centuries.  George Hall, the Gypsy Parson often met her, carrying her basket and puffing a small black pipe, and gave a vivid description.  She wore gay kerchiefs 'three or four deep, meeting on her bosom in old-time style.  Hooked like a falcon's beak, her nose drooped over her pursed lips towards a prominent chin, giving her a witch-like mien.  Quadrupled strings of corals encircled her wizened neck and a black velvet bodice bedecked with silver buttons, a skirt of bold check pattern, and a poke-bonnet formed her customary walking attire.'

Other Gypsies spanned the two centuries and like so many of their forebears and later generations seemed to be living out of their time, in the way they dressed.  Solomon and Sarah were such a couple, and Sarah, with her short plaid skirt, was simultaneously in advance of and behind the fashion.

In 1896, when Sampson first met Matthew Wood, then aged about fifty, he had glossy black ringlets reaching down to his shoulders.  When Dora Yates met him eleven or so years later, his black ringlets had turned to grey curls.  Nevertheless, he was still a striking figure in his black bowler hat, grey coat and floral velvet waistcoat, worn with short corduroy trousers, gorgeous purple stockings and high boots.  His son Harry also wore for very best, a buff coat and knickerbockers of white doeskin.

The gorgeous attire in which DORA YATES DESCRIBED VIVIDLY A MEMORABLE the four Romanies SOIREE AT LIVERPOOL UNIVERSITY IN 1903·4 had arrayed themselves was truly ATTENDED BY LURENI ALAMINA, BLANCHE & wondrous to behold, and so differ- BEATRICE BOSWELL ent from the rather shabby long skirts and draggle feathered large hats and dilapidated laced boots in which they ordinarily went dukering and monging. 'You sees, my Rawnies, we wants to do yous credit, and not shame the Rai (Sampson) in front of all

dose foolish learned ladies and gen'lemen,' Alamina
explained.
So Lureni's black satin dress positively shone with
richness and the huge golden rings in her ears must
have weighed them down intolerably. Alamina, in
gorgeous striped scarlet silk flounced from waist
to hem, and her throat and bosom hung with
row upon row of coral and gold necklaces, outshone
Cleopatra herself, while the two girls were visions
of loveliness in white and yellow with brilliant
scarves round their necks. All four wore multi-col-
oured Paisley shawls round their shoulders, and
their glossy black hair uncovered.

Isaac Gray was an equally imposing character, who bridged the centuries, in a well-cut green riding-coat decorated with handsome buttons; a yellow scarf tied in a huge bow round his neck and on his grey head a wide-awake hat, which he would doff with a flourish.

The Gypsies in their gorgeous attire, described by Dora Yates, are representative of the many others, who dressed as the occasion demanded. This is still the case.

When George Hall described a 'horde of ancient vagabonds' attending a fair, he said what particularly struck him was the motley character of the party, adding that it was an 'assembly of the quaintest rag dolls, he had ever beheld. As an admirer and friend of the Gypsies, he was not being critical, but was emphasising the varied colours and nature of their clothes.

The Gypsies had now entered the century when fashion was to change much more rapidly than before. One result was that many more outdated clothes were being discarded by gaujos and passed on to the Gypsies, either as direct gifts or in the 'rags.' After a day's tatting, the rags were tipped on the ground for sorting, and among the poorer families any wearable garments were eagerly picked out. This was always a scene of merriment, especially amongst the younger members. Sometimes two girls would make a dive for the same dress and, as each refused to let go, it usually ended torn clean in half.

Now Gypsies were faced more often with styles they did not like. Luckily some of them could sew. Thomasina Lane, who always wore a dark woollen gown with a large apron; a little red shawl pinned across her breast and a big black lace cap, was one such needlewoman. In fact, being the best in her district in Devon, she received many orders for her shirts. Some of these were of white linen, very finely tucked, and one design, which fastened behind, was embroidered between the tucks, and had additional curious little straps on the shoulders. The shirts were made according to the rank of the wearer, and some of the chiefs had gold buttons on theirs. A Gypsy would place an order on his way from one fair to another, then call for the finished garment on his return.

The skill of sewing and the increased wealth of the Gypsies gave them a new independence. They could now indulge their high standards and their personal taste to the full.

Just as the red cloaks in the nineteenth century seem to have caught the eye of the Gypsies, the apron and later the 'pinna' must be the garments most strongly associated with the Gypsy women of the twentieth. These utilitarian forms of dress became the vehicles for displaying exquisite fancy detail and style. There were two kinds of aprons (jardoxas): those worn as smart dress aprons and for out-of-doors, when hawking or standing at the ball box of a coconut shy; and the others for preparing food or for domestic purposes. The 'best' aprons, which were made of good quality black Italian cloth with a very silky appearance, were pleated at the waist or gathered in small tucks and smocked in coloured silks. The waist-band was about three inches (7.5cm) wide in the centre tapering off to about an inch (2.5cm) to form the strings at the back. They had two large patch pockets, sometimes finished with a black crochet frill around the side and bottom edges, usually in a point-pattern, and five narrow tucks at the bottom. The waist band was sometimes ornamented with rows of machine stitching, and its edges feather-stitched in light blue or cherry coloured silk, and flowers in coloured silks were embroidered on the patch pockets, the edges of which were feather-stitched to match the waist-band.

The domestic aprons were usually made of white or red lined dark blue cotton drill; or blue and white, or red and white check cotton. White working aprons were also frequently worn, made in the same style as the black ones, but without any ornamentation. Sometimes white aprons were worn for hawking, but these were far more elaborate and made in the style of the dress aprons, with a deep frill of lace or crocheting at the bottom.

Henry Lee told me that his grandmother would wear an apron in the front for working, at the same time having her best fastened behind. By this means she was immediately able to transform herself to receive guests, by pulling round the best from the back. Another system was to wear the working apron over the best, and simply hitch it up when visitors called in the same way that country people used to hitch up their aprons to reveal their skirts.

The outstanding dresses worn at the beginning of the century (circa 1910-20) were made of plush, usually coloured amber, light or dark blue, cherry or deep crimson. They were tight fitting to the waist with full skirts reaching nearly to the ankles. The neck was cut with a round yoke trimmed with white lace, and the sleeves, which were puffed to the elbow, were also finished with white lace frills. The skirt was similarly trimmed with three circular hoops of lace. Fred Huth, who married a Gypsy and who was born at the end of the nineteenth century, recalled seeing at Bridgwater Fair 'three young Gypsy women, probably sisters, all dressed in plush frocks, one amber, the second cherry and the third pale blue.' And he said 'they seemed to light up the whole fairground, like birds of paradise in a field of crows.

Often these dresses were set off by broad brimmed black hats of fine straw or beaver, trimmed with large ostrich feathers dyed the same colour as the plush dresses. And on fair days and other festive occasions the Romani women would complete their attire with white embroidered petticoats and high-legged brown boots with black stockings.

Scottish plaid was a favourite for both dresses and skirts. Red plaid dresses were usually trimmed with black velvet collars and cuffs, and three rows of black velvet round the skirt, while those in green plaid were usually trimmed with green velvet. Pleated plaid skirts became popular at a slightly later date continuing in popularity throughout the century and may still be seen today.

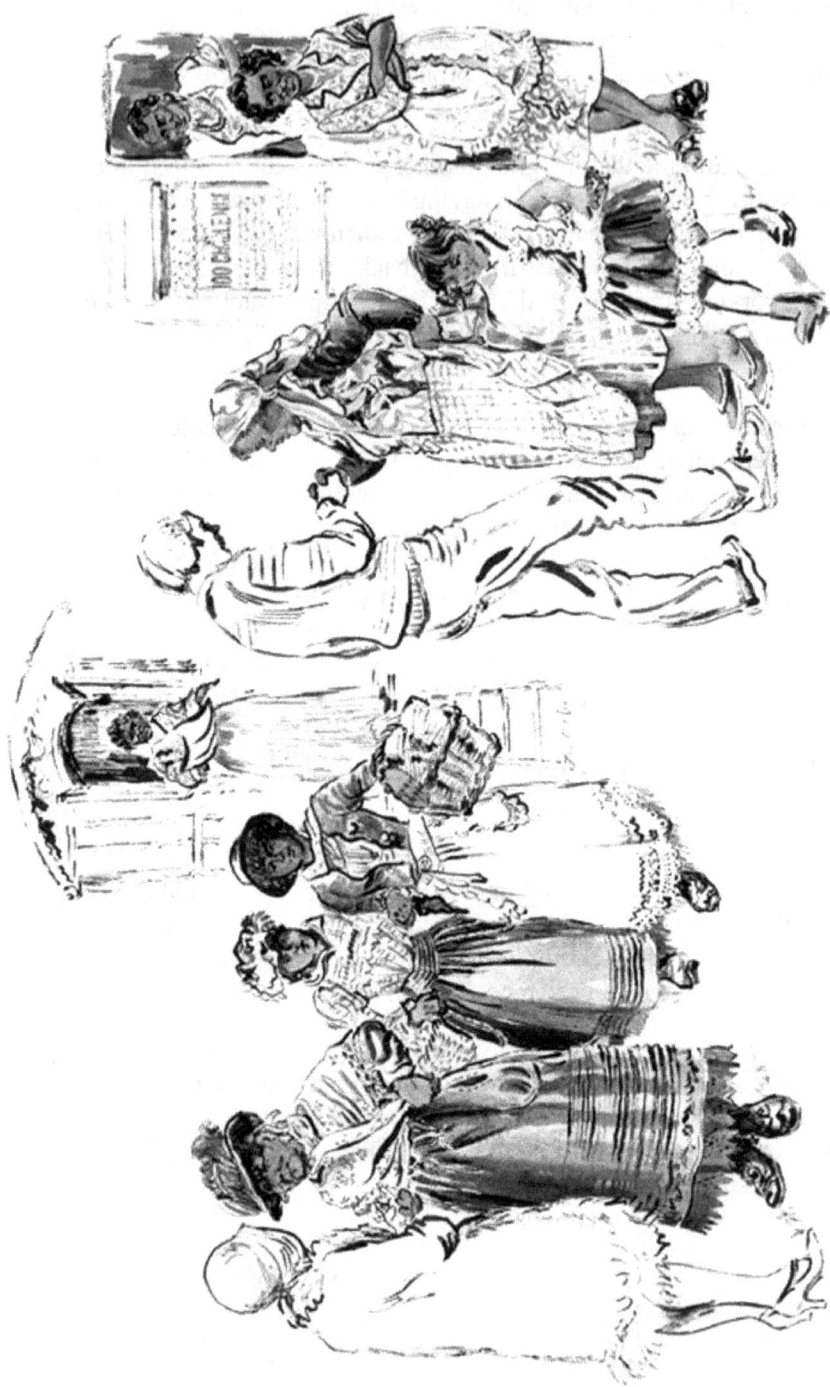

Some of the older women favoured black satin dresses made in Romani style with tight fitting bodices, full skirts and plenty of trimmings. For summer the younger women and children liked grey, blue or red and white check cotton gingham and these dresses were also cut in the traditional Gypsy fashion.

Under their skirts, the women wore red flannel or white calico petticoats (cufas) – those for best being very full and frilly. No more than two underskirts were worn and, unlike those of the foreign Gypsies, who visited England some years before, they did not have deep pockets for hiding their booty. However, a number of the older women wore under their skirts, a separate buttoned pocket made of stout linen, fastened to a waistband, to hold the money they earned by hawking or dukkering (fortune-telling).

Among the poorer families the mothers were fond of buying second-hand dance frocks for their daughters, especially those in dark coloured lace, which the girls wore for everyday wear when out hawking or at work – a practice that must have appeared strange to gaujos.

For suits, the Gypsy women preferred either black and white check, or dark brown or green tweed. The jackets (cokkas) were usually three-quarter length, fitting to the figure. Winter overcoats were always tight fitting as well, made with raised seams and some had velvet collars.

The accessories or finishing touches are well known, often being the first items to catch the eye. The gorgeous black hats with dyed ostrich plumes, similar to those worn by the Coster Pearly Queens on festive occasions, were natural successors to the beaver bonnets worn before.

North Country Tinker and Potter women often wore small round brown fur hats shaped like Russian hats, but these did not catch on in the south. A little later the women took to wearing a man's Trilby style of hat.

Silk handkerchiefs continued to be used as head-dresses, either folded in a triangle over the head and tied in a bow under the chin, or draped and tied at the back. Alternatively, diklos were worn round the neck.

Shawls (baro diklos) also continued to be worn, either full length or as 'Turn Overs', reaching to the waist only. Welsh flannel shawls were popular, usually made with white and blue lines forming checks and a

wide blue border with long fringes. Griffiths of Swansea was one noted firm that sold them. Some older women wore elaborately patterned shawls in the 'Pine Pattern, colourful Paisleys or those of fine Indian cashmere. These were fastened across the chest with massive brooches.

As always, the women's dress was set off by jewellery.

Some of the women wore very stout leather belts with large plated or brass buckles, either in brown or black leather, about two inches wide. Such belts made handy weapons if the need arose.

Little Gypsy girls dressed in the same style as their mothers. In winter they usually wore Scottish plaid dresses, in knitted jersey and plaid kilting, or velvet dresses in red, blue or brown. In summer, red or blue and white check cotton dresses were worn, while white frocks, trimmed with plenty of embroidery, were kept for best. Most of the children wore small silk handkerchiefs knotted round their necks, and red coral or amber necklaces, as well as small gold ear-rings - either plain rings or small hoops. They wore scalloped high-legged Luton boots just like their mothers. In fact, generally all small children were dressed in the same fashion as their parents. Small boys were not immune, and from four years upwards might be seen running about in long 'tail' dealer's coats and flap fronted long trousers, all stitched and seamed. This custom of dressing children in the same way as their parents was not exclusive to the Gypsies but it was taken much more seriously and continues to this day.

The men, not to be outdone, took over the three-piece suit and turned it into something typically Gypsy. While, after the Edwardian period, gaujos' suits became dull and dowdy, the Gypsy style continued to develop in its own special way.

In various parts of the country, tailors, who were able to make specialized Gypsy styles, became well-known. Some tailors made garments at their own premises, while others employed factories to fulfil orders; but, unless the factories were accustomed to making suits of this kind, a discerning eye was able to spot the difference in quality at a glance.

The old men always chose very thick, heavy cloth, usually dark brown or dark green in colour, although sometimes of a grey and white check. A putty-coloured material known as 'breeches cloth' was a great favourite, because it showed up the strapped or 'lap' seams and machine-stitched patterns more strikingly than the darker shades. Most of these heavy cloths were made in Yorkshire and were very harsh to the feel – one tailor referred to the stuff as 'bull's wool.' Kinder to the touch was the black or brown velveteen, which was also used for coats and sometimes waistcoats, but never for trousers, which were always corduroy or cloth.

Some of the older men wore long tailcoats fitted to the waist with either circular collars, sometimes faced with velveteen and buttoned up close to the throat, or else stepped (i.e. turned back) collars with lapels. The seams were either three eighths of an inch (1 cm) double stitched lap seams or five eighths of an inch (1.4 cm) strap seams. These coats were made with five outside patch pockets: two breast, one ticket and two larger side pockets. The pocket flaps were finished with five rows of stitching round them, while the pockets themselves were only double-stitched. The flaps were usually buttoned down to the pockets with single buttons. Inside, the coats had a breast pocket on the right and a poacher's pocket – large enough to hide a rabbit – on the left.

The edges of the coats were finished with five rows of stitching barely a quarter of an inch (6mm) apart, and the sleeves had an open buttoned cuff also finished with five rows of stitching. The fronts of the coats were stitched in fancy patterns. Those known as 'chain fronts' were composed of three straight rows of stitching on the outer edge and two rows inside, forming the chain. The stitching ran from the collar to the bottom of the coat and then continued along the bottom edge. The 'corkscrew' or 'barley twist' fronts had three waved inside rows of stitching with two straight outer rows. Finally, a third fancy front was ornamented by a scalloped stitched pattern – the scallop points turning in towards the buttons on one side and the buttonholes on the other. This design was usually made with just two rows of stitching, starting at the top and ending at the bottom button; the edges and the pocket flaps were only double-stitched, but there would be the usual five rows of stitching round the bottom of the coat.

The coat linings were made from lightweight, woollen cloth and the sleeves were generally lined with a silky material. This was necessary since most of the waistcoats at the time had sleeves - hence their Romani name baiengri or bangeri, a 'thing of sleeves' – and if made of velveteen, as they frequently were, they would have clung to an ordinary lining.

The buttons (krafnis) of the coats and waistcoats were often made of horn, rimmed by a silver horseshoe. The centres of the buttons sometimes represented the frogs of horses' hooves, or the head of a greyhound. These buttons were light in colour and usually reserved for light check suits or coats. For darker materials inferior composition buttons were used with the horse-shoe rims and the frog centres moulded into the buttons. Other Gypsies preferred smoke pearl buttons, and later the leather krafnis became fashionable. Coins continued to be shanked and used by the older generation but were more common on shirts.

Short lounge coats or jackets were square cut and never waisted like the tail-coats, but, like these, they either buttoned to the throat or had step collars. The pockets, seams, stitching and fancy patterned fronts were the same on both types of coat, only the backs differed. The backs of the lounge coats had a four-arched yoke across the shoulders, and a two inch (5cm) wide back-strap, ornamented with five equidistant rows of stitching running from the yoke to the bottom of the coat. This style was made with two six-inch (15.2cm) side vents. However, if a twelve-inch (30.4cm) centre vent was preferred, the back-strap would run from the collar, down over the yoke finishing at the top of the centre vent, either squared or in a point.

Some Gypsies ordered no yoke and only the back-strap, others vice versa. Velveteen jackets had less fancy stitching than those made of cloth, only having double or even single stitched 'lap' seams.

Waistcoats (baiengris) were rather long and square at the bottom. They were stitched like the coats and usually the collars and the backs matched as well. There were exceptions, when in spite of the coat having a step collar, the waistcoat had a circular one, buttoning to the throat to protect the chest to the neck, where the diklo was worn – collars and ties being unheard of in those days among Gypsies. Most of the waistcoats had sleeves with an open single button cuff, stitched to match those on the coat. The sleeves and back of the waistcoats were generally made of grey or brown speckled jean, though some Gypsies preferred black or brown velveteen. The cloth lining was similar to that of the coats, but the sleeves were lined in cotton. The backs of the waistcoats had two side vents about two inches (5cm) deep, and a centre vent like an inverted 'V.' They had a yoke and a two inch back-strap, which ended in a point just above the centre vent, as well as the usual strap and buckle for tightening the waist. They were stitched all-round the bottom, and usually the backs matched the coat. Some Gypsies used to wear brown plush waistcoats, which like the velveteen coats has little stitching and ordinary flap pockets instead of patch. In all other respects they were made in the same style as those made in cloth.

Plush waistcoats, velveteen coats and corduroy trousers were bought as separate garments and not as part of a suit.

Trousers (bulengris, rokamiaw or rokkengris) were cut high in the waist and had the old-fashioned 'whole-fall' flap fronts with seven rows of stitching round the flap, or three rows and a chain pattern like that on the coat fronts. They were usually made with a double seat for riding and a right hip patch pocket with a flap, embellished with five rows of stitching and a button. The cut of these trousers was somewhat similar to that of jodhpurs, very roomy in the seat, with wide thighs and rather tight at the knee and calf. The bottoms were always one or two inches (2.5 or 5cm) wider than the calf measurement, and some old Gypsies called them 'leg of mutton' trousers. There was a loose lap seam (i.e. the lap seam was only stitched on the inside, the outside edge being left loose like a tuck) about half an inch wide, down the outside of the leg. The two-inch turn-ups had seven rows of stitching, and if worn turned down, as they often were, might have the addition on the inside leg, of small 'scuff' patches which the Gypsies called 'kicks.' These kicks were about five inches long and shaped like a pointed shovel, (or the spade in a pack of cards) coming to a point about three inches up the leg. They were designed to take the wear off the legs brushing against each other. The trousers were always lined, usually with strong heavy unbleached calico, as underpants were seldom worn at that time.

Since the trousers wore out first, several corduroy or 'cord' trousers were required during the lifetime of one cloth coat and waistcoat. Velveteen corduroy – usually needle-cord in dark brown or black – was very popular, and another favourite was the 'Gypsy' cord, which was also velveteen but with wider ribs - some straight and some wavy. A third material, which was not velvety, was 'Worsted' cord – a narrow cord usually reddish or rust brown in colour. These corduroy trousers were made just like those in cloth except that they had a red binding round the top.

There was a tailor in Oxford, who, like his father before, made clothes for Gypsies from all over the South of England. Once he made a pair of trousers for Shipton Buckland (Shippy), who collected and took them back to the spot where he and some other Gypsies were stopping. Having put on his purchase, Shippy strutted about in front of the others, prompting one to say, "That's a nice pair of trousers you got on, my Shippy, but there is one thing wrong with them, they wants taking in at the knee about the eighth part of a barley-corn and no more." Shippy immediately climbed back into his wagon, took off the trousers, which he wrapped up and returned to the tailor. "That was a good pair of trousers you made me and I ain't a-grumbling, but they wants taking in at the knee about the eighth part of a barley-corn and no more." The tailor knew that Shippy was a bit queer in his mind at the time and agreed to have them ready next day. When the Gypsy returned, the tailor fetched the parcel and opened it for inspection. "Ah! That's better, wrap them up again." And away he went with his trousers as happy as a bee. Later the tailor said that they had never been taken from the paper until Shippy called for them!

W. Rowlingson of Bishops Stortford was another outfitter popular with the Gypsies. Edward Prior joined the shop soon after it opened in 1924 and was responsible for taking the customers' measurements. He remembered the suits, which were made up until 1941, by which time Dysons had taken over the business, which they did in 1938. The men's three-piece suits which the firm also made for boys as young as six, were mostly in brown or grey worsted. The jackets were usually single breasted and had a centre back vent, and they kept all the fancy details, essential to the Gypsy style: four patch pockets on the front and buttons of silver horseshoes, complete with nail-holes These buttons closed the jacket and both fancy cuffs were decorated with two. Sometimes there were two yokes across the back of the jacket, which was finished either with four or six rows of top stitching or quarter inch (6mm) raised seams down the front and all the way round the bottom. The collar, cuffs and pockets were also stitched.

The 'four pocket' waistcoats were either with collars or collarless, with belted backs made in a silk finish fabric. Like the jackets, they were finished with four rows of top-stitching as well as the horse-shoe buttons.

The trousers were mostly fly fronted with brace buttons. They were tight legged with six rows of stitching round the bottom and the tops were finished with a red braid. Two pockets were required inside the front of the waistband for the safe- keeping of notes.

Edward Prior had quite a problem quoting a price because so many extras were asked for. Between 1925 and 1928 a suit cost no more than four to five pounds.

Many clothiers, who catered for Gypsies, used to make up suits in several sizes for the fruit and hop picking seasons, as some Gypsies could not spare the time to have one made.

They usually asked the tailor if he had a 'misfit set of clothes' to sell cheap, and of course he was able to oblige with a so-called misfit from his made-up stock. Providing the style was right, fit was a secondary consideration because the Gypsies were getting a bargain. The following anecdote exemplifies the indifference some Gypsies had to the fit of their clothes.

Fred Huth saw on Epsom Downs, a small boy running about wearing a pair of man's trousers, the top of which came up so high that they were tied round his neck with string, while the legs stretched several inches beyond his toes, so that he kept falling down. His father called him saying, "Take them trousers off, boy, them's a bit long for you." The boy pulled them off and his father took his billhook and chopped off the ends to what he thought a suitable length.

As well as the clothes that the Gypsies had specially made, they used to 'mong' (beg) or buy 'left offs' from gaujos. Among those favoured were the coachmen's livery overcoats, made in fawn-coloured, finest quality box-cloth, with the crested buttons, which were removed and replaced by pearl ones. They also liked the blue Melton top-coats that bookmakers wore; the black cloth overcoats with astrakhan collars and cuffs, worn by doctors or actors; the huntsmen's red waistcoats, or the game keepers' old brown velveteen tail-coats, and the check riding breeches and box-cloth gaiters of other sporting characters. Even an old lady's umbrella covered in black silk might provide a grinder or 'mush-faker' with a neckerchief. To complete their outfits, the Gypsies chose their own style of shirts (gads). The most common were made of red and green plaid flannel, with red as the ground colour and the pattern in green.

The fronts, shoulder-seams and cuffs were feather-stitched in yellow, and sometimes small Canadian gold coins were used as buttons. One of the well-known makers of these shirts, who had a shop in Worcester Street, Birmingham, used to receive orders from all over the country. Some shirts of finer material had smocked fronts as well as featherstitching. Usually these were ordinary readymade shirts with the fancy needlework added by the Gypsy women.

The men were just as particular about the finishing sartorial touches as the women. Several styles of hats and caps (stadis and hufas) were popular. The black or buff coloured box hat, narrowing towards the crown, was worn a great deal in the first quarter of the twentieth century, as well as the straight-brimmed, hard felt bowler, with a high crown and air-vent eyelets in the sides. Sometimes a sporting Romani would decorate his bowler by putting in the hat band the ear of a hare caught by his lurcher. Another hat often seen was the cast-off grey silk or white beaver topper of some statesman or racehorse owner, like the one which Scamp wore. Later, the soft black velour 'Trilby' came into fashion – usually worn with the crown dented out at the top.

Caps were common including the brown plush hufas with earflaps, which tied over the crown with a tape, in a bow, while the back turned down over the neck. Jack Musty, a lean raw-boned man, with short side whiskers, who stood over six feet in height, usually wore a brown plush cap, a yellow neckerchief with white spots, a reefer jacket, corduroy breeches and box-cloth gaiters. The Gypsy youths favoured the Ted Sloan caps, named after the jockey. These had very long squarish peaks and were usually in a check pattern.

The neckerchief (diklo), which came in numerous colours and patterns, remained a very important feature of their dress. One of bright yellow with white spots varying in size from that of a shilling to a small pea, with a two inch (5cm) white border was very popular. This pattern was also made with a ground colour of light royal blue or chocolate maroon. The 'snowstorm' was another pattern. This was borderless, in dark navy blue, covered with white spots of four different sizes from that of a large pea to a bird's eye, resembling large and small snowflakes. Then there was the diamond pattern, usually in chocolate maroon, which had small white diamonds and white rings in clusters, with a large red diamond here and there. A shop in the Bull Ring, Birmingham was well known for these neckerchiefs and most pawnbrokers in large cities stocked them new and not pledged. A good diklo was always to be found at the pawnbrokers in Old Market Street, Bristol, and in Hounslow, Middlesex. A great number were manufactured at a silk factory in Leek, Staffordshire, so some Gypsies called them Staffordshire handkerchiefs, and a few of the yellow diklos with white spots and borders at one time came from France.

Some Gypsies always washed a new handkerchief before wearing it to take out the dressing and soften the silk, and they never allowed a hot iron to be used because they believe this made the silk perishable - they would only have them pressed.

These neckerchiefs were dual purpose. If the man had no proper slips for slipping his greyhound after a hare, it was customary to take off the diklo and thread it through the dog's collar, holding one end firm and letting go of the other, when the dog (jukel) sighted the hare.

Fred Huth, who supplied most of the details of this important period up to circa 1920, said that the Gypsy style of dress was not, except in the case of fortune-telling, an asset for making a living and that this possibly caused its disappearance. He said it was impossible to put a fixed period to the style, but as time passed it became increasingly subdued, and a marked change took place when the Gypsies became motorized. Nevertheless, a few old 'standard' Gypsies continued to dress in this fashion until at least the Fifties.

Mr Huth described the dress as becoming 'more subdued' speaking from that period. Looking back, one cannot wholeheartedly agree, although some suits did become less detailed. It is understandable that the passing of a picturesque period might be mistaken for a passing fashion. But the Gypsies did not and do not have to be old-fashioned to keep their style. They soon discovered the benefits, when gaujo fashions became in some ways more practical and comfortable to wear, and so the men's suits followed the general trend by becoming a little more relaxed in cut. The fall fronts gave way to the fly opening, and the collared high-necked waistcoat gave way to the V-neck, which was also worn in the nineteenth century. The fancy details, which were the essential element in their style, such as scalloped backs and top stitching remained popular. Even when suits became less extravagant in fancy-work, they were never as subdued as those of the gaujo.

The outfits of the roaring twenties must have surprised both Mr Huth and the Gypsy women, but this did not prevent the young and adventurous from adopting the cloche hats, low waistlines and short skirts, making them look every bit as zippy as women of fashion. Nonetheless, they still appeared quaint beside the gaujos, partly because of the continued practice of using party dresses for day wear, or by being in some measure out of date.

The one garment, which initially seemed out of character with Gypsies, was the bib and brace - notable for its plainness and practicality. However, when realized that it was worn by the country and western idol, Jimmie Rodgers in the 1929 film 'The Singing Brakeman,' the bib and brace assumes an entirely different macho image, well suited to Gypsy men.

In 1940, Croft Cooke visited Pershore Horse Fair and shared a similar experience to the Gypsy Parson at the beginning of that century:

'Who were those strange dark horsey men whom I remember seeing that day? They were dressed in clothes which might have escaped notice in individual cases yet were somewhat fantastic as the wear of a multitude – buttoned leggings, antiquated panama hats, flowered waistcoats, black coats which buttoned high on the chest such as no tailor has made in this century. And I remember an odd miscellany of male jewellery, silver watch-chains with links like tie-rings, great gold pins in stocks and neckerchiefs, turnip watches and an albert or two. There were whiskers and beards of ancient styles and figures which might have stepped from a Morland print. I swear that when I picture Pershore Horse Fair it seems to have called its crowd not from the surrounding country but from the past century.'

This colourful description endorses the point that, apart from the bib and brace, the Gypsies successfully resisted the dowdy trends after the Edwardian period.

Fred Huth lamented that the younger generation had discarded the old style of dressing 'and in many cases, instead of wearing an ordinary business suit, had adopted the horrible 'Spiv' style, with plimsoll shoes of a hideous design and an 'Arthur English' Spiv tie with a scantily clad ballet dancer on it, 'but,' he continued, 'thank goodness, up to now I have not seen a young Romanical in a 'Teddy Boy' outfit.'

Mr Huth was in for a great surprise.

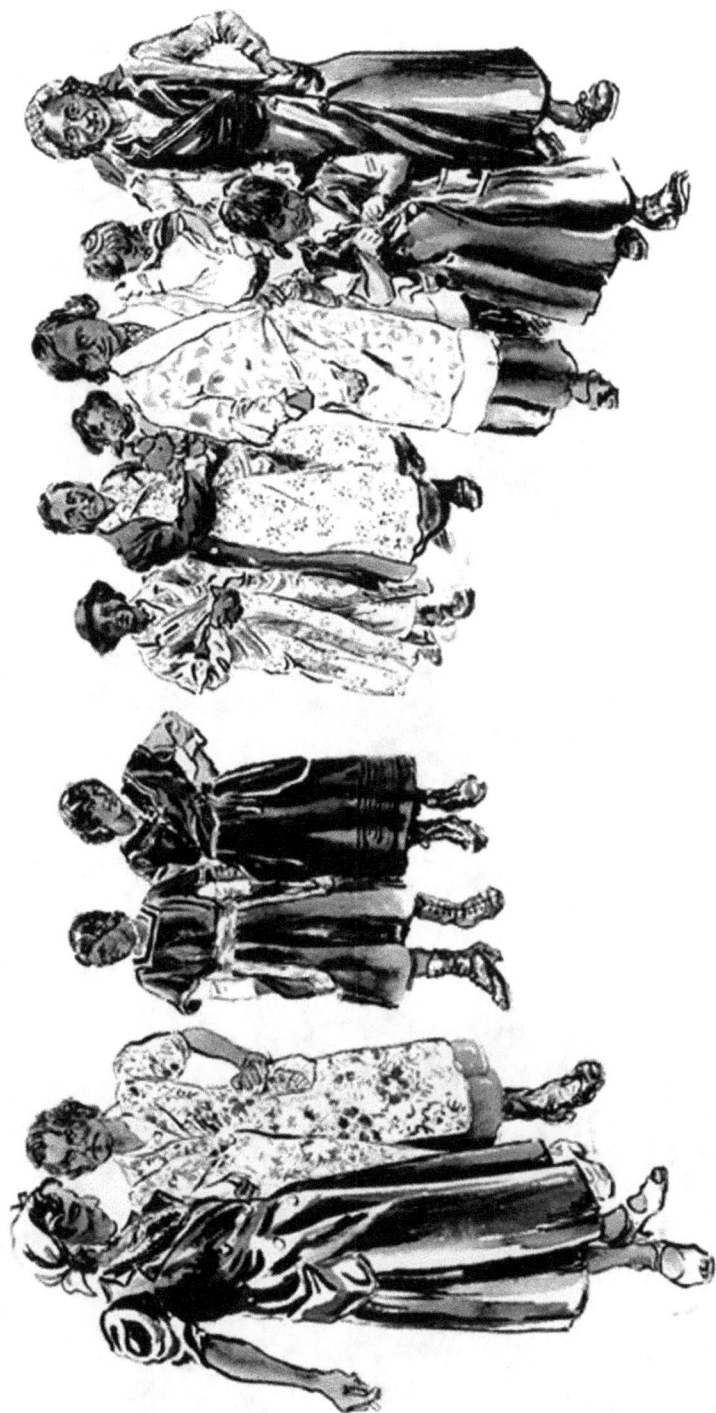

The following decades saw the Gypsies making them peculiarly their own.

Women started to wear overalls in factories in 1916, during the First World War.

## VIII  THE NEW DAWN

### Forties on and into the twenty-first century

Fred Huth had no need to mourn the demise of the old style of dress. Despite the ever-increasing changes in twentieth and twenty-first century fashion, the Gypsy look remained constant, because they continued to be governed by their own tradition and taste. The main difference was that they were now five, instead of fifty years behind the time.

From the late Thirties, the cinema accelerated the Gypsies' awareness of fashion, particularly among the young, who were enthralled by the sartorial styles of American gangsters and cowboys. The 'Spiv' or 'American gangster' style of suit – often in striped worsted, with padded shoulders, pleated seams, abnormally baggy trousers and distinguishing hat – was not so alien to Gypsy tradition as Mr Huth thought. It had the dramatic, virile qualities that Gypsies demanded, and they soon discovered this, some even abandoning their knotted diklos for American ties.

The Cowboy fashion, which followed, was at the height of its popularity during the second half of the Forties to the early Fifties. Western singers like Gene Autrey and Hank Williams, who followed Jimmie Rodgers – the earliest and most enduringly popular of these singers – were greatly admired by the Gypsies and their clothes were equally admired, so much so that they are still being worn. Not only is this tradition kept alive by stars such as Don Williams and Dolly Parton, it is a tradition which suits the Gypsy men and women down to the ground.

Elvis Presley was without doubt one of the greatest stars of the century and the Gypsies appreciated him as much as anybody. Even while Fred Huth was writing, some Gypsies had already embraced Elvis's look and adopted the Teddy Boy fashion. The greased back hair with the D-A, the velvet collars on wide shouldered, well-fitting jackets, and the exaggerated tight drainpipe trousers conformed – as did the Cowboy fashion – to the Gypsy tradition. True to form, these suits were often given a Gypsy twist being worn with diklos and turned down Wellington boots. Although some of the girls wore luminous socks, these and crepe shoes were not readily adopted.

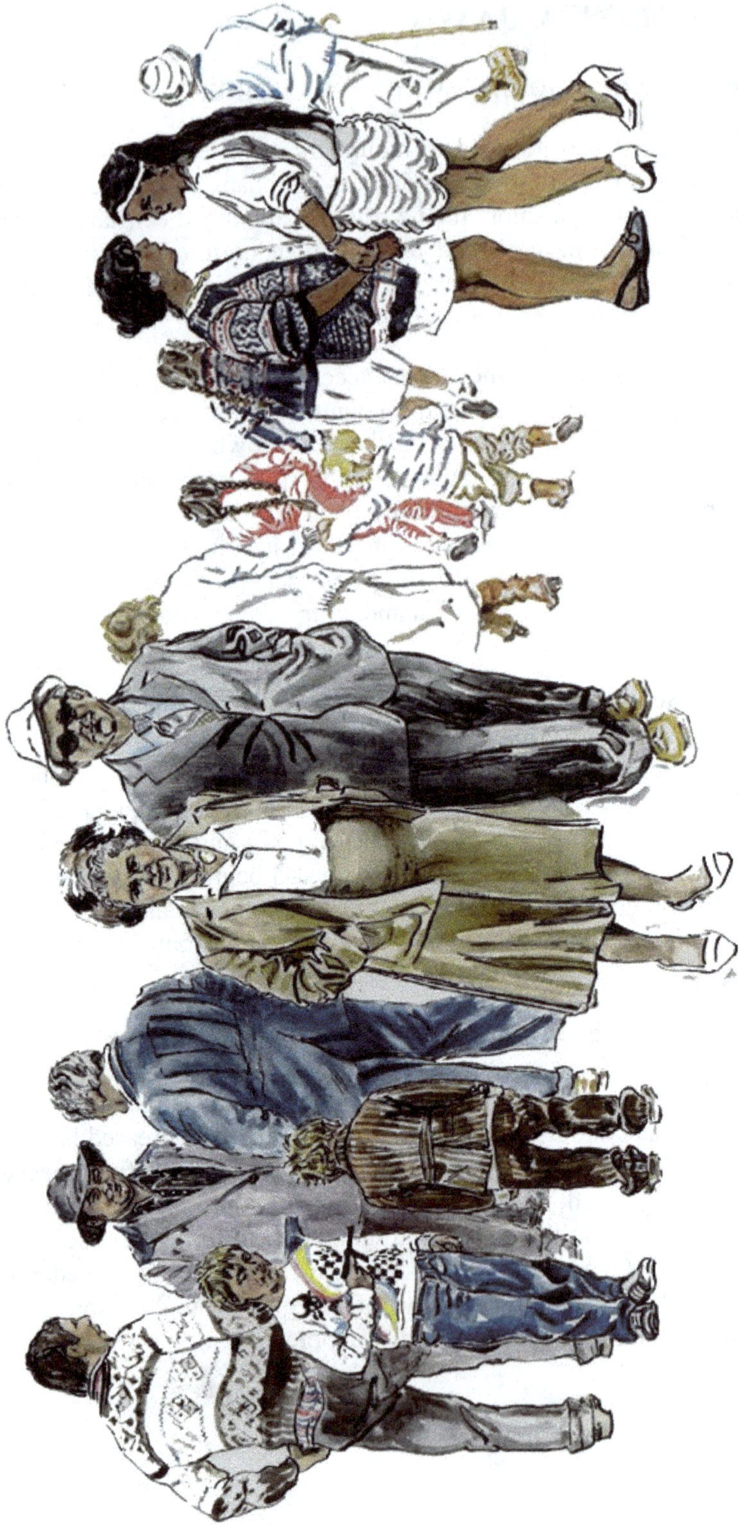

The Teddy Boy fashion, which was at its peak between 1954-1958 was most popular with the Gypsies from 1957-63, showing a marked decrease in the time taken to adopt a style compared to the previous century. Elvis's hairstyle was almost standard with the men, particularly the young, from the late Fifties to the mid Seventies, with the exception of some flash Gypsies, who often wore their hair parted and shorter from the Sixties onwards.

To any visitor, a Fair day around the end of the Fifties would have produced a similar miscellany to that which had confronted the Gypsy Parson and Croft-Cooke before, with its clash of colours and extravaganza of fabrics and fashions. The women dressed in frills and full-skirted frocks – varied in length, sometimes several worn over each other and topped with the ever popular 'pinna,' together with their valuable beads and brooches, as well as gold or silver rings in the ears and on their hands. Even more conservative, the older women in button boots and the little girls dressed in lace or broderie anglaise, Victorian style frocks. Coloured handkerchiefs or diklos, patterned with diamonds and squares, or spots, would also be seen covering the women's soap greased hair and knotted around the necks of the men, who would have been as varied in their styles as the women. Some men wore tailor made Gypsy suits, modern versions of those worn earlier in the century; others looked as if they had just walked off the silver screen, in wide-shouldered striped worsted suits, American ties and snap-brim hats worn far back on their heads; while some of the youths dressed in second-hand 'drape' suits. All of these outfits – in varying degrees – were out of their time.

Moving on, the men's suits of the Sixties to Seventies have been described as a cross between old style Gypsy suits and those of Teddy boys in the Fifties. As before they were made according to the individual's preference. The jackets were longer than those worn by gaujos, but not as long as those of the drape suits. The backs varied but most of them had raised stitched yolk backs like the Cowboys or those worn earlier. They were sometimes pleated with a sewn in half-belt, or a loose buttoned-on belt, while others simply had either single or double vents. Dark fabrics, generally dark blue or black, were usually chosen to show up the numerous mother-of-pearl buttons. The flaps of the four or five pockets were all buttoned, and the cuffs, which might be quite fancy, each displayed six. A turned back triangular shaped cuff embellished with six pearl buttons looked especially good. The collars were sometimes velvet, matching the flashy light colours of the jacket lining, whereas the lapels were not matched. The trousers had raised

double stitched seams down the legs and round the slant pockets, unusual for the time - hipsters being the thing amongst gaujos.

A 'Gentlemen's bespoke tailor' from the north, employed by Gypsies from 1969, said that they never wanted to see the style books or take advice as they knew precisely what they wanted. In fact, he found them very hard to please – undoubtedly because of their exacting standards. They always supplied their own cloth – not difficult in the area – and by this time were to some extent following fashion, which might determine details like the lapels. The major visible difference was the big easy fitting jackets with wide shoulders, which allowed plenty of room for thick jumpers or cardigans. The trousers, in both length and width, were not unusual for the time, while their two front cash pockets were – but these were an understandable necessity for Gypsies.

Although this tailor was not asked for scalloped backs, fancy cuffs, or to make up suits for children, these, along with the three-piece suit remained popular, particularly the tailored suits for children, which are still popular today.

The overall or 'dealer's coat', adopted by Gypsy men and worn until the late twentieth century seems almost as unusual an item as the bib and

brace. Generally, of brown or grey denim, they resembled - and in some cases probably were – the overalls worn by carpenters and tradesmen.

As suggested by the name, they were most commonly worn at horse fairs and auctions. In contrast to the wearing of gold, which inspires the confidence of their own kind, the adoption of this conservative style may have been to inspire the confidence of the gaujos, who would be dealing at the sales as well.

The women also adopted the overall or pinafore, but they made their 'pinna,' like the apron, peculiarly Gypsy by a glorious extravagance of

Circa 1983

detail. Wartime blackout or cotton sateen were the most favoured materials for these garments, which were styled with pleats and tucks, and decorated with rows of stitching as well as embroidery and feather-stitching to embellish the large horse-shoe pockets. They certainly knew how to put glamour into working clothes.

During this century, while the handkerchief continued to be an important part of women's dress, the shawl of the women gradually gave way to the cardigan. By the Eighties, knitwear had taken on a new lease of life in the fashion world, displaying increasingly complicated patterns and designs. Two of the most distinctive styles might have been especially designed for the Gypsies.

Both men and women naturally took to the geometrically, patterned cardigan, with bands of zig-zags, checks and crosses familiar to them from old Welsh blankets of the previous century, or the patterns of their early history. Yet more interesting was a design unwittingly devised by a top knitwear designer, who little realized that the globular bunches of grapes and cherries which brightly festooned the woollies of her design might have been picked off the surface of a Gypsy 'van. Soon these cardigans were to be seen in great numbers on the Gypsy women and little girls. This particular design, which appeared in the designer's knitting book of 1981, also appeared in a women's magazine, and shortly afterwards a few knitters were kept frantically busy fulfilling orders.

Another design known as 'intralux,' resembling the weave of Gypsy baskets was adopted a little later, but it was not nearly as popular as the grapes and cherries, which were still going strong after this design disappeared.

When faux fur yarns appeared on the market, this was right up the Gypsy girl's street, and towards the end of the Eighties it became popular, as did mohair, which has remained a winner to this day. The mohair cardigans were and are often finished with rolled edges entwined with gold or silver thread, and usually embellished with sequins and satin motifs – those for the children often being clowns. As well as these decorated mohair cardigans, in the second half of the Eighties, jackets of materials such as denim received similar treatment, though less sophisticated. The treatment of these was more on the wacky side, using leather shapes and strips of fur for the appliqué.

Appliqué together with embellishment are so in keeping with the Gypsies' taste that it is seen on all types of garments, from the casual to the smart, and as the twentieth century drew to a close these clothes became available in the shops and markets.

Leather and furs have always been part of the Gypsies wardrobe and the twentieth and twenty first century have been no exception. The fashionable leather suit designed for gaujos might equally well have been designed for the Gypsies.

In the early part of this century (2004), mink became the rage. It was and is worn by all ages, and usually made up into ankle length coats, but also as shorter coats or jerkins. Typically, these might be worn on a sunny summer's day, and why not, who would want to be parted from such a stunning garment? At the same time cashmere capes trimmed with fox fur became popular, as well as cashmere and fox jackets. It can be no surprise that these furs remain popular.

A long mink coat would cost close to £2000 and a cashmere shawl about £500, which proves that Gypsies are not afraid to pay for luxury. This point was well hammered home by the television series 'Big Fat Gypsy Weddings,' which highlighted the truly remarkable and luxurious dresses made by the talented and canny Thelma Madine and her team.

Today, while many of the older generations have scarcely changed their way of dressing and remain behind the times, there are as many who, along with the young, are abreast with them. Over the years Gypsies have gradually caught up with fashion and by the Seventies, when Traveller Education had become the norm, the young had more or less caught up. So why do they still stand out in a crowd? One reason is their taste for the exotic demands a degree of exaggeration – be it brighter or darker, fuller, tighter, longer or shorter – or worn in a slightly different way. Their taste always makes its stamp.

The mink coats worn by the women and little girls are not only worn longer but they are worn according to the occasion rather than the weather, such as at a fair on a blisteringly hot June day. In contrast, on a cold, wet day young Gypsy girls will wear the scantiest sequinned clothes like those gaujo girls might wear at a night-club. This principle applies to shoes as well. Although you will see trendy patterned wellingtons, there will be just as many pairs of glitzy shoes with heels of

exaggerated proportions suitable for Hollywood stars at the Oscars but worn by Gypsies at a wet and muddy fair.

If we visit a fair today, our impression will be much the same as before. This impression will not be diminished by the fact that we have become used to great variety in fashion – a variety, which has increased as the centuries have progressed. This vast variety has had repercussions on the Gypsies' guise as well, and so today and no doubt tomorrow, we shall still see a mix of styles past and present, exaggerated or worn in an unusual way.

At the fair we shall see Gypsies every bit as beautiful as those described in years past. They'll be splendid in their voluminous, brightly patterned and zanily styled skirts, frills, pinnas, scarves and jewellery, fit for Royalty. Others will be wearing fur coats – fake or real, leather suits, slinky trousers, crops or jeans, pencil skirts or baring their richly tanned legs and mid-rifts below and above the scantiest mini-skirts. And in contrast there will be long dresses – some so slinky and dazzling they would throw a footballer's wife, dressed to kill, into the deepest shade.

The males add to the assortment in no mean way. Their suits and separate trousers and jackets are long or short, wide or narrow, dark or pale, maybe checked or striped, often held up with colourful braces, while others might simply wear jeans, jogging trousers, long shorts or crops - totally abreast of fashion.

We'll see tartan and patterned shirts, geometrically patterned cardigans or coloured diklos – although these are being abandoned as the Gypsies notice that gaujos are adopting them. Some might be in leather or sheepskin coats, but, unlike the women, not worn regardless of the weather. And there'll be an extensive range of headwear from Homburgs to Trilbies, Panamas to Cowboys' Stetsons and assorted caps: and on their feet – dealers' boots, wellingtons, brogues or weary looking trainers, to name but a few.

To add to the razzle-dazzle, gold will gleam from both the men and women. There will be heavy chains, carrying coins or heavy pendants such as horses or large crucifixes, denoting that many are born again Christians; bulky and ornate gold rings, sometimes on several fingers, as well as huge gold rings dangling from the women's ears. And proving that they are thoroughly up to date, some of the young girls abandon gold for brightly coloured costume jewellery.

The children are a treat for the eyes whether they are in rough and ready outfits; fashionably chic, sporty outfits; or decked out - the girls in their frills and furs or, like the boys, emulating their parents in tailored suits. As for the babies in prams, at times both are so frilly it is hard to know where the baby ends, and the pram begins.

Words cannot express the thrill of the spectacle.

A gentleman gave a pair of his trousers to a Gypsy. A week or so later, when out walking, he saw a small Gypsy boy coming towards him & 'there seemed,' said he when relating the occurrence to me, 'something very familiar about this boy's dress, which at first puzzled me considerably; but afterwards, as the boy came nearer, I saw that he had made a complete suit from my old trousers; a little had been cut from the legs, the pockets had been turned inside out and the ends cut open, so that by getting into the garment and thrusting his arms through the pockets, as sleeves· he secured a sort of combination suit, trousers and coat in one; he had reduced the opening at the top by tying pieces of string from button to button, and to complete the garment and separate what I may perhaps call the blouse part from the trousers portion, he had tied a piece of cord around his waist.' Now the boy was small and thin and the gentleman to whom the trousers had belonged was of somewhat ample proportions, therefore the appearance of the boy, it is

perhaps needless to add, was more ludicrous than can
be well described, reminding one of the account given by
Gypsy Smith of his first pair of trousers, which
prompted inquiries as to whether he was going or coming, at what time the balloon was going up, and so on.

FRANK CUTTRISS

114

# CONCLUSION

The Gypsies do the same for themselves as dress designers do for gaujos – they adopt and adapt. In the past some adopted and adapted out of need, but now few have that need allowing flexibility and choice. Unlike gaujos, they are not bound by any convention of fashion or the style of a peer group, but they are bound by their own taste dictated by their historical background, as I hope has been proved.

At times it is still necessary for them to merge into the community, just as it was centuries ago. The paradox now is that the Gypsy man may disguise himself in sober dress to instil trust in others and gain employment, while his dukkering (fortune-telling) wife will be decked out in all her finery, making public her Gypsy guise to instil the same trust.

Important as the cut of the cloth is, Gypsies are more attracted by colour and decoration. It is the eye-catching which pleases – whether spotted horses or spotted diklos.

Their attitude to dress gives the Gypsies a timeless quality, as well as revealing their inherent pride and way of life. Their nomadic life has enabled them to walk anywhere with an easy, unconscious, confidence, whereas gaujos – especially on strange ground – seldom have this ability. The Gypsies' glance, their posture and movement and above all their aura, can make items of dress appear peculiar to them even when they are not. What passes unnoticed on gaujos can seem remarkable on Gypsies, often demanding another look.

This is beautifully described by Rupert Croft Cooke:

'There is a way they have of wearing clothes as if with a certain contempt, and yet not failing in effect. A man in ragged jacket and trousers with heavy 'traveller's' boots and a collarless shirt will pull on a worn cap over one ear to let a mass of ringlets fall over the other and so give himself a jaunty look. A woman will use a flash of blinding colour such as no gaujo woman would dare to wear. They have a kind of natural elegance which never leaves them.'

Truly it may be said of the Gypsy: 'It ain't what you wear, it's the way that you wear it.'

1982 and 1983

1983 and 1984

2009

# BITS AND BOBS

Elynour Rummynge

C16 quotes

An Act of 1597

Lazzie Smith and his family

Taboos about cleanliness

Funeral Dress

Confirmation Dress

Jewellery

Hairstyles

Boots

Children's Dress:  Suits

Braces and Belts

# ELYNOUR RUMMYNGE

Her Kyrtel Brystow red;
HER BODICE AND SKIRT COMBINED BRISTOL RED;
With clothes upon her hed
That wey a sowe of led,
THAT WEIGH A SOW (OR PIG) OF LED,
Wrythen in wonder wyse,
WOUND IN A WONDERFUL WAY,
After the Sarasyns gyse,
With a whyn wham,
WITH A ROUND REVOLVING TABLE,
Knyt with a trym tram,
KNIT WITH A TRIFLE,
Upon her brayne pan
Like an Egyptian
Capped about
When she go out.          John Skelton circa 1517

This is a small part of Skelton's poem The Tunning of Elynour Rummynge.
Elynour ran a public house and was not a Gypsy although Skelton depicted
her dressing like one. His description of her headwear is clearly that of the
mysterious 'bern', seen in Bosch's painting of the same period 'The
Haywain.' Chapters 1 & 11

Thomas Harman also mentions the headdress in a prefix to the 1567, 3rd
edition of a Caveat or Warning for Common Cursitors referring to the 'wily
wandering vagabonds calling & naming themselves Egiptians, deeply
dissembling & long hiding & covering their deceitful practices – feeding the
rude common people, wholly addicted and given to novelties, toys & new
inventions, delighting them with the strangeness of the attire of their heads,
and practising palmistry to such as would know their fortunes.'

Shortly before 1550, Dr. Andrew Borde recorded the earliest example of
Romanes in The Fyrst Boke of the Introduction of Knowledge, first
published circa 1547 and again circa 1562, by William Copeland,
Fleetestrete & Lothbury. In Chapter xxxviii he writes of the Egyptians,
their money and speech. He also refers to their dress or disguise, already
noted in some of the Acts. Borde writes:

'The people of the coutry be swarte and doth go disgisid in theyr apparel
contrary to other nacions, they be lyght fingerd and vse pyking (picking
pockets) they haue little maner, ad euyl loggying and yet they be
pleasant dausers. Therbe few or none of the Egipcios y doth dwel i egipt

for Egipt is repleted now Wt infidel alyons. Ther mony is brasse and golde yf there be any man y wyl learn part of theyr speche Englyshe and Egipt speche foloweth.'

The Chapter is illustrated with a woodcut of a man wearing a cloak and a headdress, which is probably meant to be a turban, but looks more like a shower cap, or in Thompson's words a Pyrenean beret. This woodcut was also used to illustrate other chapters and so it would be a mistake to assume it represents a Gypsy.

Reference: Borde's Egipt Speche by Henry Thomas Crofton
Journal Gypsy Lore Society New Series Vol.I No.2 October 1907

---

1597 Act 11 And be it also further enacted by the authority aforesaid, that all persons calling themselves scholars, going about begging; (2) all seafaring men pretending losses of their ships or goods on the sea, going about the country begging; (3) all idle persons going about in any country either begging, or using any subtle craft or unlawful games or plays, or feigning themselves to have knowledge of physiognomy, palmistry or other like crafty science, or pretending that they can tell destinies, fortunes or such other like fantastical imaginations; (4) all persons that be, or utter themselves to be proctors, procurers, patent gatherers, or collectors for goals, prisons or hospitals; (5) all fencers, bearwards, common players of interludes, & minstrels wandering abroad (other than players of interludes, belonging to any baron of this realm, or any other honourable person.

age of greater degree, to be authorized to play, under the hand & seal of arms of such baron or per-
sonage) (6) all jugglers, tinkers, pedlars and
petty-chapmen wandering abroad; (7) all wand-
wandering persons and common labourers, being
persons able in body, using loitering, & refusing to
work for such reasonable wages as is taxed or commonly given in such parts where such persons do or
shall happen to dwell or abide, not having living
otherwise to maintain themselves; (8) all persons
delivered out of goals that beg for their fees, or otherwise do travel begging; (9) all such persons as
shall wander abroad begging, pretending losses by
fire or otherwise; and all such persons not being
felons, wandering and pretending themselves to be
Egyptians, or wandering in the habit, form or attire
of counterfeit Egyptians, (10) shall be taken, adjud-
ged & deemed rogues, vagabonds & sturdy beggars,
and shall sustain all pain & punishment, as by
this Act is in that behalf appointed.

Lazzie Smith, and his family at the Liverpool Exhibition 1886

Lazzie Smith    Margaret Smith    Alice Smiith    Cecilia Smith    Nathan Lee
Ernest Smith    Midora and child    Kerlenda Smith    and Wallace Boswell

Although the Gypsies were staying in a bender tent, they were dressed for
the occasion, which may have surprised the gaujo visitors. Midora and the
little girl doubtlessly caused an even greater stir. They went to town and
wore gloves.

# TABOOS ABOUT CLEANLINESS

Amongst the taboos relating to cleanliness, the Gypsies have always kept a separate bowl for washing clothes and would not dream of using the same bowl for vegetables. One can't help wishing that this practice was universal amongst gaujos. They went even further, insisting on men's clothes being washed apart from women's and on their being packed separately for travelling. To comply with the former rule, the women often did their own washing in a waterproof hole at some little distance from the camp, usually out of sight. Thompson related that old Ezekiel Lock, who died about 1914-5, insisted on women's and babies' clothes being washed after the men's in running water, or in a different bowl, and on having separate wallets to carry them on the donkey. In common with other Gypsies, he would not allow women to step over food or food vessels, or to hold bread against their clothes, when cutting it, unless they had put on clean aprons. All of this sounds reasonable but would seem more so, if the women were making the stance.

Although the Gypsies shared the same attitude towards cleanliness, their prohibitions and precautions were not necessarily identical from family to family. Nonetheless, the precautions always discriminated against the women. During periods of menstruation and childbirth, further taboos unrelated to dress occurred.

Although the washing machine has done much to undermine these taboos, stainless steel or fancy plastic washing bowls are still sold in sets of three.

# FUNERAL DRESS

In the fourteenth century, black became generally recognised as symbolic of grief and mourning, and its association with funerals is so strong that the use of another colour now seems strange. However, when the Gypsies used white as a funeral colour in the nineteenth century, they were merely continuing the oldest and most widespread of customs. They were not alone for it is still worn in India, parts of Europe and elsewhere. Although it is tempting to assume that they had brought this tradition from India, it was almost certainly picked up nearer home as, in the nineteenth century, it was still used by some country people in England.

As a symbol of virginity and innocence, white had been used by gaujos at funerals both for and by maidens (sometimes old ones) and children, for a long time. White palls, favours and scarves were even used for bachelors in the seventeenth and eighteenth centuries. During the last forty years of the eighteenth century there was a relaxation for those gaujos committed to black in that children began to wear white with black trimmings.

The wearing of white by the Gypsy men, as it had been for gaujos, was generally restricted to accessories such as white ribbons in their black hat-bands, white neckties and white gloves. This particularly applied to gaujos mourning the death of an 'innocence.'

When Sinaminti Buckland was buried, eight girls dressed in white held a white sheet instead of a pall, the deceased being considered 'young and single,' although she was the mother of at least five children. In bright contrast, she was followed to her grave by Gypsy women in red cloaks and smoking pipes.

Repronia Lee, known as the Gypsy Queen, was unmarried when she went to her grave at Kesgrave in 1862. Her sisters and girl cousins wore white muslin frocks, corded with white silk and their heads were covered with white veils reaching almost to the ground. Hundreds of Gypsies from all parts of the country attended the funeral, all clad in white. The men's black silk hat-bands were tied with white ribbons and they wore white gloves and neckties.

The Gypsies were neither bound by conventions, nor bound to be different. In 1851 at the burial of John Chilcott junior at Kesgrave, 'the mourners were few, but they were decently attired in black.' (Suffolk Chronicle) A panel on his tomb shows two men in top hats, representing

John and his younger brother either side of a horse. John was a horse-dealer.

Now, most Gypsies would feel that it is only decent to dress in black, its use having become quite common amongst them by the middle of the twentieth century, and many are unaware of the colours used by their ancestors. At a funeral in 1984, on seeing a mourner wearing brilliant green accessories, an old Gypsy woman scornfully commented 'They'll be wearing white next!'

While white symbolises the purity of the soul, red represents the blood of Christ. Red has also been used as a mourning colour for a very long time. In the seventeenth century deep red survived as a mourning colour but not in elegant gaujo circles, and even towards the end of the nineteenth century in England, deep red was deemed a proper alternative to black, during the mourning period after the funeral. Whereas, in the nineteenth and twentieth centuries, some Gypsies still used red for the ceremony and this was unusual. Several instances of Gypsy women wearing red cloaks to funerals – sometimes new for the occasion – as well as children dressed in red, are recorded late in the nineteenth century. Even at the turn of the century, at a funeral near Old Romney, much red was evident in the women's dress and some of the men wore red diklos similar to that worn by the deceased. Many Gypsies told Thompson (a Gypsy aficionado) that red was formerly the mourning colour for women, and some said that it was for men also. Of course, this may not have been universal, since at the time they were not travelling the length and breadth of the country so customs varied at variable rates. The colour possibly persisted until the Forties in Britain as it was recorded as late as 1945 for the dressing of a Gypsy corpse in the States. Apparently, the men used to wear red rosettes, or ribbons in their buttonholes or pinned to their coat lapels. When Matilda, wife of Levi Stanley, who emigrated to America about 1860, was interred at Dayton, Ohio in 1878, red was the predominant hue of the funeral trappings; each mourner wearing a scrap of crimson, and the hearse decked with red plumes.

Customs such as the Scottish Gypsy rite of laying a circle of red and blue ribbons on the dead; the painting of the tombstones at Yatton, red, white and blue; and the fastening of ribbons to a rose tree growing on Louis Boswell's grave, suggest that red may have been considered a prophylactic colour as it was with the Greek Gypsies, although the Gypsies in Britain do not seem to have given any such superstitious reasons.

The colour red was not confined to the mourners or restricted to favours for the dead. Louis Lovell was buried in a suit of red flannel and Eliza Heron wore a scarlet cloak and bonnet. In 1924 Levi Boswell was buried wearing a muffler of brilliant red, while on his feet he wore bright yellow socks.

In 1931 at the funeral of John Sampson, the Gypsies were gaily dressed. It seems that the deceased and the mourning Gypsies were often gaily dressed in both the nineteenth and early twentieth centuries, predating those gaujos who chose to celebrate the life of the deceased in gay colours today.

The practice of burying people in their ordinary or best day clothes was not widespread, but more commonplace among Gypsies than gaujos. Some Gypsies went so far as to struggle into their best clothes before dying to avoid gaujos seeing or touching their naked bodies. A different explanation was given to a north country doctor, when visiting a dying Gypsy chief, whom he found dressed in all his robes of state. He was told 'if our king is going to meet the King of Heaven, is it not right that he should meet him as a king?'

Evidently this practice, which occurred in Germany and Eastern Europe too, inspired the confidence of the dying and was considered to add dignity as well as giving greater comfort and a better preparation for the journey.

Covering the head does not seem to have been common. Apart from Eliza Heron's scarlet bonnet, Eliza Boss of Derby was buried with the hood of her cloak turned up. The only other known cases refer to the wearing of unusually arranged kerchiefs by Lovinia, Ambrose Smith's daughter; Deloraifi, Lawrence Boswell's daughter (dec. 1885); and, strangely enough, Tom Brown, a Norfolk Gypsy.

On the other hand, Scottish Gypsies of the nineteenth century and even before seemed to have taken the head more seriously than the body. A paper cap was used and paper put round the feet, leaving the body bare except for a circle of red and blue ribbons, similar to the variegated cockade worn in the hats of newly enlisted recruits in the army, which was placed on the breast opposite the heart.

In England, the Derby Boswells regarded the custom of being buried in shoes as common in the days of their parents and grandparents. However, this custom does seem to have been mainly confined to the Midlands. Outside this area only two cases appear to be recorded: Celia Chilcott wore satin shoes when buried in Kesgrave, and red morocco slippers were worn by Jack Lee of Brighton, who died in 1899. A notable record is that of Absolom Smith, who was buried in 1826 wearing shoes adorned with silver buckles each weighing half a pound. In 1839 Louis Boswell was buried fully dressed, shod in buckle shoes, and later that year his daughter Vashti was buried also fully dressed and wearing buckle shoes. Round her waist was a broad belt ornamented with silver and having concealed pockets in which money had been placed.

Vashti was not alone in departing well prepared. It was a common practice to enclose a few necessities or comforts for the next life and clothes were the commonest. Ethelenda Heron's coffin contained her entire wardrobe, Sentinia Smith's the better part of hers, and Savaina Lovell's one or two dresses, a silk shawl, and other bits of finery. These Gypsies and many more besides were interred only in under-garments and a shroud, with the extra provision of some or all of their clothes. The burial of extra clothes, when the deceased were dressed was probably a little less usual, although several Gypsies spoke of it being customary once.

The provision of footwear was clearly not customary as there are only three known cases, and one of these is most unusual: Job Cooper was buried with a new pair of shoes and seems to have been the only Gypsy provided with something wearable yet unworn. The burial of Theophilus Boswell in Derby in 1872 was more conventional: His very large coffin was almost filled with clothes but his suit, fresh from the tailor, was omitted and cut up to send to a rag shop.

While the Gypsies may have felt extra footwear unnecessary for the next life, they appeared to think a dead man might miss his watch and a woman her jewellery. The Derby Boswells regarded stripping a dead woman of her jewellery as both wicked and dangerous. They generally placed any trinkets not worn at the death with the deceased in her coffin. Other Gypsies battered up the unworn jewellery and either dropped it in water, or buried it in a hole or beneath the coffin. At the Old Romney funeral, the widow removed her gold wedding ring and replaced it with one of silver. She then tied the original ring to her husband's left wrist with a scarlet ribbon.

A curious custom carried into the twentieth century was the turning of clothes inside out. This practice, which was known in Bulgarian mourning, could have originated in South Eastern Europe but as no similar rite seems to be recorded for continental Gypsies, it was probably derived from folklore at home. A belief was recorded in

Shropshire that in certain places the devil exerted influence over travellers, and with most success in narrow or difficult ways. A village stile was his favourite spot for harassing unfortunate travellers, where efforts to clamber over would be futile until the poor individual turned some article of clothing inside out. So strong was this superstition that some women deliberately turned their gowns before crossing a stile.

A simple explanation may have been that the devil was no more than a robber hoping to find money in the inside pockets.

The Gypsies found another unlikely use for this extraordinary custom. Johnny Winters told that if his old Daddy was lost, he turned his coat inside out and put it on again. Apparently, it wasn't long before he found the right road – leastways that was his story. And Taiso Young, when incapable of finding his camp on one festive occasion, is said to have solved his problem by this method; while the Irishman of one of Mrs O'Connor Boswell's stories extended the practice to all his clothes, which enabled him to find his way home after being carried off by the fairies into a strange country.

Some Gypsies took the practice yet further.

Isaac Heron, who died in 1911, was buried clothed in pants, socks and a starched white linen shirt. Before his body was laid in the coffin, Iza, a relation, put in one suit of best clothes and a good overcoat, all turned inside out. He then covered them with a striped bed-cover. When Iza was handling the clothes before putting them in the coffin, a clinking or rattling sounding like money or something metallic was heard, but Iza would not tell what was in the pockets. Two other members of Isaac's family are known to be buried with their clothes turned inside out and laid with them in this way. In other instances, the turned clothes were worn – a custom familiar to some Gypsies, while others denied its regular use. Piramus Gray, a son-in-law of 'No Name' Heron, was interred in full walking dress with his coat turned inside out. And in Oxfordshire, Agnes Smith thought that the underclothes on a corpse were always turned inside out, as they were at her brother-in-law's funeral in 1907.

Did the Gypsies believe that this curious custom, which was so successful on earth, would offer the same assistance to the spirits travelling into the mysterious realm of the next world?

The Gypsies' concern did not end with the journey since they were anxious that their departed kindred should rest in peace. Many believed that the souls of the dead would revisit former habitations and cling to their earthly possessions if given the opportunity. To avoid such a possibility the possessions were destroyed – usually by fire. Excepting the Woods, who became Roman Catholic and abandoned funeral sacrifices, and some Gypsies who had mixed with gaujo blood, it seems to have been an invariable rule that clothing not enclosed in the coffin should be destroyed as well.

Nonetheless, there were odd instances. One was known of Coralina Loveridge (née Boswell), who kept her sister-in-law's red cloak for a keepsake. There were also the exceptions of the chests in which clothes of the deceased were kept, as described by the Scottish tinker, Murray. (see chapter VI) Since Sampson, who was renowned for his Gypsy knowledge, accepted that these chests and their contents had belonged to Gypsies, it is hard to question the statement. At the same time, it is hard not to, as it is known that on the Scottish borders, the Kirk Yetholm Gypsies burnt the deceased's clothes, convinced that wearing them would shorten the days of the living.

When a child died, it was not customary to destroy anything other than the clothes.

The Gypsies were convinced that fate would befall them, if they did not adhere to their custom, which allowed the departed to rest in peace. Delenda Williams, referring particularly to personal belongings, averred that anything used by the dead was not fit for the living to have and those keeping them were 'putting themselves in the way of trouble, and must expect to come to an undateful end!' And Lavinia Boswell foresaw a host of misfortunes as the lot of those who retained a dead relative's clothes or personal possessions: "You'd be haunted and daunted with bad luck and disease into all your days. You'd have no rejoicement – and whatsoever you did it'd prove a curse to you. And maybe you'd go out of your mind, or maybe you'd waste away into a skeleton. And nobody would associate with you or your kinspeople: your sister, you had been brought up with would not know the side of the road you were on. 'Bide away from them', she would tell her husband and children, 'for they are under a curse, that'll pass on to we and we mix and mingle with."

On a more cheerful note – dressed for Confirmation, 2009 – Gypsies believe
that this ceremony is worth dressing up for.

# JEWELLERY

Frank Cuttriss and Fred Huth, writing in 1915 and 1960, left little to add to the subject of jewellery and personal adornment from the late eighteenth century. They believed, as this book sets out to prove, that the Gypsies' love of jewellery, brilliantly coloured fabrics and the ability to use them artistically or unusually was inherited from their Oriental forebears. A Gypsy allowed Cuttriss to examine and feel the weight of her curious large gold earrings, which she suggested were old Indian work. He was convinced.

Jewellery from before the outset of the nineteenth century left a lasting impression, as does that of today. Much of it was very old, having been handed down through the generations, while other pieces were, and still are, striking in their size or design. The greatest number of ear-rings of this time were crescent shaped, consisting of either a single crescent or a combination of several. It seems probable that this design had the reputation of being lucky since some early Egyptian earrings were of this form, and the crescent is also used as a religious symbol. However the real origin is obscure.

In Eastern countries much larger earrings were worn than was customary in Europe, and although large ones were sometimes worn by the Gypsies, smaller ones, from the plain circles of gold wire to elaborate silver of gold drops, were favoured. The largest earrings seen by Cuttriss on a Gypsy consisted of mainly long, angular drops, between three or four inches (7.5 - 10 cm) long, ornamented by a sunk panel in each of the faces (Fig 1). Such was the length of these rings, they only just cleared the shoulders. This length would not be so unusual today.

Many of the little girls wore and still wear earrings. In those days they were mostly silver and occasionally gold, whereas today they are rarely other than gold.

Nearly all the women, young or old, wore necklaces. Beads were very popular, especially black or red – lucky colours. Also popular were cowrie shaped beads (Fig 2), which Cuttriss thought gave grounds to suppose that these shells might have been supplanted by beads, giving way firstly to coral. In Egypt cowrie shells were considered preservatives against the evil eye and one can only suppose that the Gypsies were of the same opinion. The size of the beads varied from an eighth of an inch (3mm) to an inch (2.5cm) or more in length by three quarters of an inch (2cm) in diameter. Cuttriss thought that if one traced back to the eighteen-eighties, the source of many of these beads would have been a place known to the Gypsies as Kaulo Gav (Black town), otherwise Birmingham. There, genuine Hindu, Egyptian and similar work could be found. Other beads would have been passed on through generations and having examined some of these, it was not beyond the imagination of Cuttriss that they were made and acquired in the Far East.

Necklace beads were either graduated; regularly varied in size, or appeared to have no order or arrangement, as if composed of portions of several necklaces. The only apparent rule was that each Gypsy wore as many rows as she had beads for – the less fortunate wearing one, while the fortunate might wear up to six – but two or three rows were more usual.

Cuttriss described a brooch worn by Mrs Petrulengro, which was a stag's horn mounted with silver. It appeared always to have been worn as a brooch but matched in every detail, the charms worn on horse-hair cords around the necks of Spanish Gypsy children to ward off the evil eye. He reminded Mr and Mrs Petrulengro that in Egypt cowrie shells had been used in the same way and for the same purpose. Mr Petrulengo responded excitedly that he knew someone with a watch-chain made of silver cowries.

Mrs Petrulengro then showed Cuttriss a circular brooch with a loose silver coin set in it. It was a piece of Turkish money, covered with writing, which, since it could not be understood, seemed to give a particular appeal to the Gypsies.

Fred Huth remembered the jewellery in the period following. He noted that whenever Gypsy women purchased jewellery that with an Oriental or 'quaint' appearance was invariably selected. Heavy buckle rings in plain gold, slightly over half an inch wide (12mm) and weighing about two ounces were usually chosen for wedding rings. Another favourite ring design bore two snake heads with coloured stones for the eyes. Other styles – chiefly massive and old fashioned – were also worn. Single and double buckle rings have remained popular and horseshoe rings make an appropriate addition.

The earrings of the early and mid-nineteenth century also remain much the same today. Then as now, large gold hoop earrings, or those made from spade guineas followed by sovereigns and other gold coins were worn, while some of the older women preferred long heavy drop earrings of both simple and elaborate designs. The little girls wore, as they still do, small light hoops of gold in their ears.

Sometimes during fights and family feuds, earrings would be torn out, but they were soon replaced – even if another hole had to be pierced in the ear-lobe. Old Maireni Smith, wife of Black Joby Smith had in her ear-lobes several marks where her earrings had been torn out when kuring. (kooring – fighting)

During the greatest part of the nineteenth century, no Gypsy woman or girl would be seen without a necklace or string of beads. These were nearly always coral, but amber was also worn. If the necklace was a single row, the beads were usually large, but some Gypsies preferred three to five strings of smaller corals twisted round the neck. When a silk diklo was worn round the neck, the corals would hang loosely over it. During the twentieth century gold chains carrying coins as pendants were popular as they are today. Sometimes there might be a couple of coins to one chain or two or three chains each carrying a coin or some other gold pendant, depending of the wealth or whim or the wearer. However they were never heavily laden like the coin necklaces worn by the foreign Gypsy coppersmiths, who visited England from 1911 to 1913.

Brooches or clasps that fastened the shawl across the chest were elaborate. Some were composed of various coloured stones or one large stone set in a silver frame. Another design was made from a five shilling piece enamelled in different colours and mounted on a pin, and there was an interlocked ring design in plain gold. Ivory cameo brooches – often very fine specimens – were also popular. These may still be seen.

Now, as in the time of which Cuttriss and Huth wrote, Gypsy women and girls are rarely seen without some form of ornament. Coins – often elaborately mounted – remain one of the most popular components of jewellery for the ears, necks or hands. The men also wear rings with coins, and buckle rings – sometimes heavy – are still popular with both sexes, but particularly men. Around the neck heavy gold chains carrying chunky gold pendants such as mounted coins, large crucifixes or horses are also worn by both sexes. The women sometimes wear several of these, while the men usually stop at one.

The young girls as well as wearing valuable jewellery, carry off with equal panache the brightly coloured inexpensive beads and earrings available today. All ages remain a visual feast.

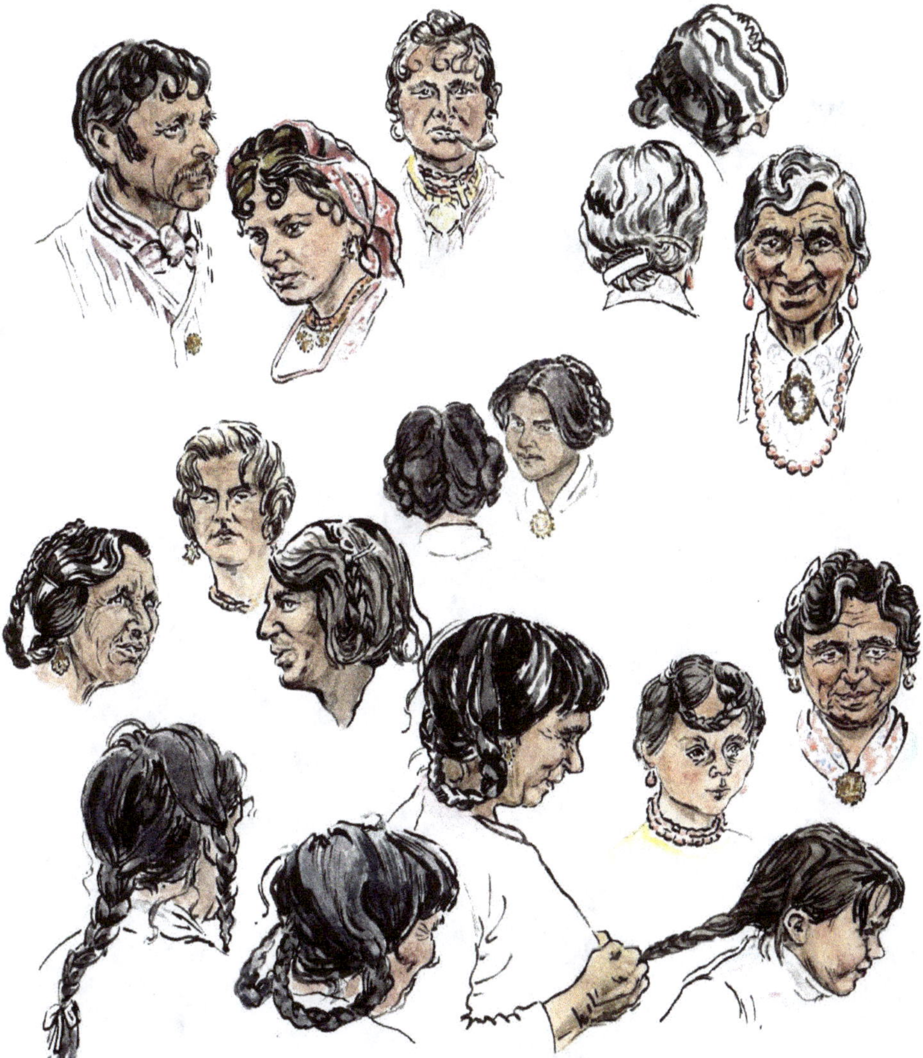

# HAIRSTYLES

We can again turn to Cuttriss and Huth for descriptions of the hairstyles from the late eighteenth century to the 1960s, and style was not just the domain of the women.

The men showed equal pride in their glossy black ringlets or fringed forelocks; others cultivated the curls of the rural labourer while quite often the young men and lads wore their hair closely cropped. It seems that then as now, the young men preferred the latest styles. One Gypsy told Cuttriss that short hair was cleaner in warm weather and his wife cut it with the horse-clippers. Usually in a camp, there was a man handy with scissors and a razor, who saved others of the community visits to the barber.

Cuttriss told of the women's distinct and artistic hairstyles, which, due to their intricacies and the extreme length of hair, took considerable time to dress. Having asked one Gypsy how she kept her hair in such perfect condition, he was invited to watch the procedure. A child was sent to fetch a bucket of water from a nearby spring, while the woman loosed many tiny plaits so that her very long hair fell like a black cascade and lay on the ground where she sat. She then wetted her hair thoroughly by holding her head over the pail and plying the brush, which was now and again plunged into the water. It was then partly towel dried leaving the breeze to do the rest, before rubbing in as much grease as possible and then removing the excess with a brush. Any grease was used, but in this instance dripping – not hedgehog fat, which was often said to be used by the Gypsies. In the absence of grease, a damp bar of soap made a good alternative. The next step was the plaiting, which was done with such speed that Cuttriss was unable to follow the process. Five plaits1 were made beginning near each ear and meeting behind the head in a series of 'door knockers,' as well as several smaller ones. Cuttriss found it all a revelation.

During this period, some of the girls and younger women wore flowers in the hair, or small sprays of foliage, when flowers were unobtainable. Later, Huth tells that tortoiseshell side-combs decorated with imitation diamonds were worn in the hair, which was always plaited, either done up in a bun at the back of the head, or hanging loosely in loops and braided. Croft Cooke described the complex styles worn by Cinny and her daughters, when they dressed up for a Saturday night out in the early Forties. They had plaits round the ears; knots at each side of the head; a small plait dropping across the forehead with its end caught in a bun over the eye, and a shining curled fringe or falling ringlets.

While many women preferred to keep their intricate plaits, others had already adopted the finger waves of the Twenties and some of the young went as far as sacrificing their locks for the fashionable bob. Soapy water was used to set the waves and combs helped to hold the hair in place. Later in the last century, when coloured plastic combs became available, they were sometimes worn, usually by the young, instead of tortoiseshell. Decorative imitation tortoiseshell, coloured or sparkling slides and combs have remained popular as have ribbons and bobbles for the children. Today a few older women, while keeping their hair long, continue to dress it into waves. Ringlets have never been completely abandoned either, but tend to be seen on children.

Alongside the older styles, styles are still drawn from current gaujo fashions – the requisite being that they show the hair off to great advantage. Whatever the style, it will invariably be more striking on a Gypsy and this goes for both sexes.

The men through the years have paid attention to their hair and slicked it into waves, curls, quiffs and DAs with grease or water. Some Gypsy men – usually the older – felt these styles were too modern. Will Taylor was one of these and in the nineteen-eighties his hair fell in loose black ringlets over his shoulders. He eventually had it cut, but still wore

it longer than was usual for the time. Today most mature Gypsy men continue to wear their hair slicked into shape and more often than not, it is their style that distinguishes them from the boring heads of their gaujo counterparts. On the other hand, unlike their elders, the youths, young boys and even toddlers wear their hair in the latest gaujo fashion.

PRICE LIST OF

# Fancy Boots

## H. LAWSON & SONS

### 19 Manchester Street

### LUTON, Beds.

# BOOTS

In the eighteenth century, Grellmann wrote 'Nothing pleases an Hungarian Gypsy so much as a pair of yellow boots.'

From early times Gypsies have extended their sartorial interest to their feet, and there have always been styles to suit their taste. The buckle shoes of previous centuries gave them the chance to vent their flamboyance in bigger and better buckles; and, as horsemen, they have not wanted for riding boots, including the cowboys' boots of our time.

Towards the end of the nineteenth century suitable footwear fell out of fashion and common use, making it difficult for the Gypsies to obtain boots, so they had to find bootmakers able to fulfil their needs. Luton, Bedfordshire had such a firm and gave the original Gypsy boots their name.

Harry Lawson ran a bespoke boot and shoemaking business from about 1875 until 1949. According to his grand-daughter who helped in the shop from 1935, it was soon after opening that some Gypsies came into his shop and asked for boots to be made to match the woodwork and patterns on their wagons. Arthur Mooring thought that it was between 1887-1890, when his father worked for Harry Lawson that the two men devised the style to meet the Gypsies' specifications. The Luton boot, which evolved, matched perfectly the scalloping and fancy stitchwork on the suit jackets of that time, rather than the patterns on the wagons. The success of the style was shown by the fact that in 1891, W. Mooring started his own business and was later joined by his son in 1919.

The favoured style had a Derby front, making the boot easier to pull on and off. It had a butterfly toe-cap, a scalloped golosh and the lacing was also accentuated by scalloping down the front. The top edge of the boot was usually scalloped and all the scalloping was enhanced by the punched design, now associated with brogues. Brass or sometimes white eyelets were requested for the laces and some old boys demanded them along the toecaps and the sides, while the buttons were beautiful pearl – red, black, brown or amber coloured.

The popular colours were a red brown called Tony red (now known as Ox-blood) or an orange-brown. Two tone was also favoured, and orders for black front and golosh with brown, scarlet, Tony red or yellow uppers were frequently received. On the occasion of the Jubilee of George V, a Gypsy man asked for a pair of boots in red, white and blue. Mooring and Son made them with the front and golosh in Tony red, the top leg in blue and the facings white. As well as the different colours, patent leather was sometimes chosen.

Women and children, as young as three or four, also wore these Luton Boots.

Another style favoured by the men was the Elastic Side boot, which came in after the Derby. The characteristic butterfly toe-cap was retained but the scalloped golosh differed in that it now went around the front of the boot. It had front as well as back straps, about one inch (2.5cm) wide. Sometimes these boots were ordered in black and tan.

The Brogue and Balmoral styles with the closed fronts were far less popular than the other two, although sometimes asked for.

Not only were the Gypsies particular about style, they also specified certain requirements to ensure the longevity and sturdiness of their boots. These included a solid leather inner sole to which the middle sole was riveted, and to this the outer sole had to be similarly riveted. Stitching was not used because it rotted in the wet grass, although occasionally, to make absolutely certain, it was used as well. In addition to the rivets, the sole part of the outer sole had brads for hard wear and sometimes three or four rows of hob-nails were also required. The heels were strengthened with an iron tip. Leather laces were used on the very heavy boots and mohair on the others.

The women ordered either Luton or Button boots with low or more usually high leg, which came up to the calf about 12-14 inches (30.5-35.5cm) from the heel. A piece of string measuring the circumference of the calf came with the orders. The Luton Button boot had the butterfly toe-cap and scalloped golosh, which continued around the front like the men's Elastic Side style, and like both other styles the black and brown combination was often preferred. No doubt the Elastic Side was not adopted because it was unsuitable for a high legged boot. However, Mooring and Son supplied gaujo women with plainer versions of the style.

The orders, accompanied by postal orders, usually came by post from all over the British Isles including Ireland. These orders were expected to be supplied within a week but usually took a fortnight, and during the 1914 war the Gypsies had to wait up to a month. Between 1890-1914 a pair cost from 8s.11d to 10s.6d (44.5p-52.5p), which was almost as much as wealthy and fashionable gaujos were paying for a pair of shoes or boots. Nonetheless, the Luton boots were exceptionally good value considering how fancy they were and that they were handmade except for the use of a Bradbury machine in the making of the uppers.

Between 1900-1914, W. Mooring and Son were turning out two to three dozen pairs of boots a week, but during the Second World War, as might be expected, trade fell off and never really picked up again although a few stalwarts continued to send orders until about 1952-4.

In the Twenties a new supplier of boots was found in Ireland. The Travellers at the Curragh wore a style that suited the baggy turn-up trousers of the period. Tutty's Hand-Made Shoes Ltd., whose business at Naas was conveniently near the racecourse, supplied Gypsies and Irish Travellers for years. Their Cattle Dealers' boots were notable for features which made them more serviceable for sloppy ground. The welt (where upper meets the sole) of approximately half an inch (13mm) with two rows of stitching was good for going over mud and slush, while the belloused tongue enabled the wearer to stand in 3-4 inches of water without getting his feet wet. Waxed thread was used for all the structural stitching to withstand these conditions. Another characteristic feature, retained on the boots was two rows of slugging (tiny nails or sprigs, approximately a quarter of an inch apart) on the heel. These boots were calf-height (Sylvester), lace ups with squarish toes. They had three rows of stitching at the top of the leg, but no punched designs, which it was thought would lead to leaks. A loop at the back and a space between the third and fourth of eight eyelets aided their pulling on and off. Like the Luton boots, they were of best quality leather.

Gerry Bray, who dealt in Cattle Dealers' boots, remembered an order for a bright green pair, but generally the older men wore dark brown or black, while the younger men chose light tan. During the height of their popularity in the Thirties and Forties, when he was young, 'You weren't anybody if you hadn't high front trousers with wide braces under which the diklo was tucked, and Cattle boots. The bottom of the trousers met the top of the boots exactly.'

Although the sturdiness of the Cattle boots was an obvious asset and a stylish contrast to the Luton boots, it made them heavy for running the horses. By the Thirties, Gypsies had discovered Quant and Son of Newmarket, (1879-1979), who were renowned for their riding boots. With its horse fairs, racing, and plenty of work on the land, roads or buildings, Newmarket was a good area for Gypsies and so the firm was well placed for their custom. Mr Bartholomew, who joined Quants in 1936 said there were always Gypsy customers in the shop. He remembered them in the old days with their black hats, suits with tight trousers, and the gold watches and chains in their waistcoats.

The Elastic Side Jodphur boots came in the late Twenties when jodhpurs started to be worn by racing people instead of breeches and leggings, but even up to 1939 they were not worn very widely by racing or farming men. These boots were always much sought after by the Gypsies but were heavier than those the racing boys required. The heavyweight Elastic Side boots known as Dealers' boots were not introduced to Quants' stock list until 1967. Those with punched or brogue toe-caps and two-tone colours were favoured, but the firm could only afford to stock the ever-popular yellow Dealers' boots. Lace boots were always in stock, but only the lighter weight Balmoral style – preferred by the racing men – had the punched toe-cap. Farmers, and of course Gypsies, who did not ride so much but still required a high leg boot, tended to choose the heavier Derby boot.

Boots continued in popularity for children and Quants stocked them from size small 9 to size 2. The Gypsies tried to get them smaller, but the little ones were unlucky. In Quants, the Gypsies found the quality of the Luton boot, though sadly it had become uneconomic for the firm to equal the decoration. However, despite inflation the same good value demanded by the Gypsies was given. In 1936 the Elastic side boot was £1.5s.9d (£1.34p) a pair, in 1968, £6.17s.6d (£6.87p), and in the Eighties, when Quants changed ownership, ceasing to cater for this specialist market, they were still reasonably priced.

Loake Bros. of Kettering was another firm who, in the middle decades of the last century, produced boots to the Gypsy taste.

Today, factories are still turning out boots for the Gypsy trade, and though they do not equal their forerunners in decoration or quality, they have style and still meet the required standard of value. It is to the Gypsies' credit that this style has evolved to a point where it is factory made, even catering for small children.

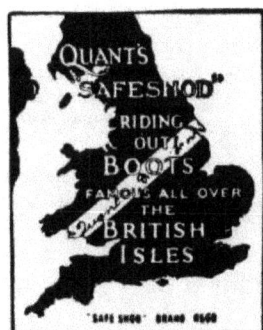

## " SAFE SHOD RANGE "

The Boots on which our Good Name has been built.

Easily the finest value in our range.

## ELASTIC SIDE JODHPUR BOOTS

Sizes & half sizes 2 to 11

### Ideal for Schooling or Jodhpur Wear

Made with strong elastic sides - easily replaced when worn - A thoroughly sturdy boot

| Prices | £ | s. | d. |
|---|---|---|---|
| Light Tan Best Quality | 8 | 17 | 6 |
| Brown Calf | 4 | 19 | 6 |
| Black Calf | 4 | 19 | 6 |

#### For Winter Wear
Sheepskin Lined Medium and Wide Fittings

Sizes 4 to 11     Price £5 19 6

STRAP JODHPUR BOOTS    To Order

Sizes and half sizes 4 to 11 — Finest leather throughout

| Prices | £ | s. | d. |
|---|---|---|---|
| Best Brown Calf | 8 | 12 | 6 |
| Brown     ,, | 5 | 5 | 0 |
| Black Calf | 5 | 5 | 0 |
| Brown Grain Neolite Soles | 4 | 10 | 6 |
| Brown Grain Waterproof | 8 | 17 | 9 |

Postage 4/6

## Quant & Son 1967

### SAFE-SHOD AND DRY SHOD

| BROWN GRAIN | £8 17 9 |
|---|---|
| Absolutely Waterproof | Sizes 5 to 11 |

#### " LET IT RAIN "

Sample Boot sent on approval  -  4/6 postage
Postage 4/6 extra on all prices.

We send C.O.D. if required

Cash refunded if you are not perfectly satisfied.

# BUI'S BOOTS

I was a-stoppin' by C---- for de fair dere, Noar, an' I 'ad five wery fine mares all in foal. An' on de mornin' of de fair I says to my Savaina: "Savaina," I says, "I'll just a-go over to de fair, an' buy anuder mare in foal, an den I shall 'ave six."

So I went over to de fair, an' bought a big black mare off'n a wery despec'able farmer, Master Pearson. "I was deturnin' wid dese here six mares in foal, an' you knows where de old 'olla tree is by de cross-roads, Noar; a man rushed out'n dere. "Your money or your life," 'e says. "I ar'n't got no money," I says, "leastways, exceptin' fifty pounds wud of five-shillin' pieces in my shoes." Den up com'd de hangman. "Dis man was a-tryin' to rob me, Master Clark," I says. "Yes, I knows, Mr Simpronius Bohemius Boswell," he says, "I 'eard 'im."

An' I goes on, an' I sees my Savaina a-top of de big 'ill a waitin' for me. "So you've come back, my Bowi," she says. "Yes, my Savaina," I says. "Come along o'me. We'll just a-go an' 'ave a glass o' beer." So we goes into de big Public an' I orders a drop o' beer for me an' my Savaina. "I ar'n't got no money to pay for it, Master Johnson," I says. "But I knows you 'ave, Mr Simpronius Bohemius Boswell," 'e says. "War'n't I a-tellin' you as I ar'n't got none today, "I says. "Mr Boswell, you always 'aves plenty of money, so don't go tellin' me as you ar'n't enough money to pay for two glasses o' beer." Dereupon off I takes one shoe, an' empties a hundred crowns onto de table; den off I takes de oder shoe an' empties anoder hundred crowns onto de table. "Dere den, Master Johnson," I says, "Dat'll buy all de beer you 'as on de premises." An' so it would.     T. W. Thompson GLSJ New S's 4

Lawson (Mooring) Derby fronted women' button boots and men's closed front below. Top right: women's boots and below right men's Derby (open) fronted boots and closed front elastic sided boots. In Mooring's time the Gypsies called them Luton or Travellers' boots.

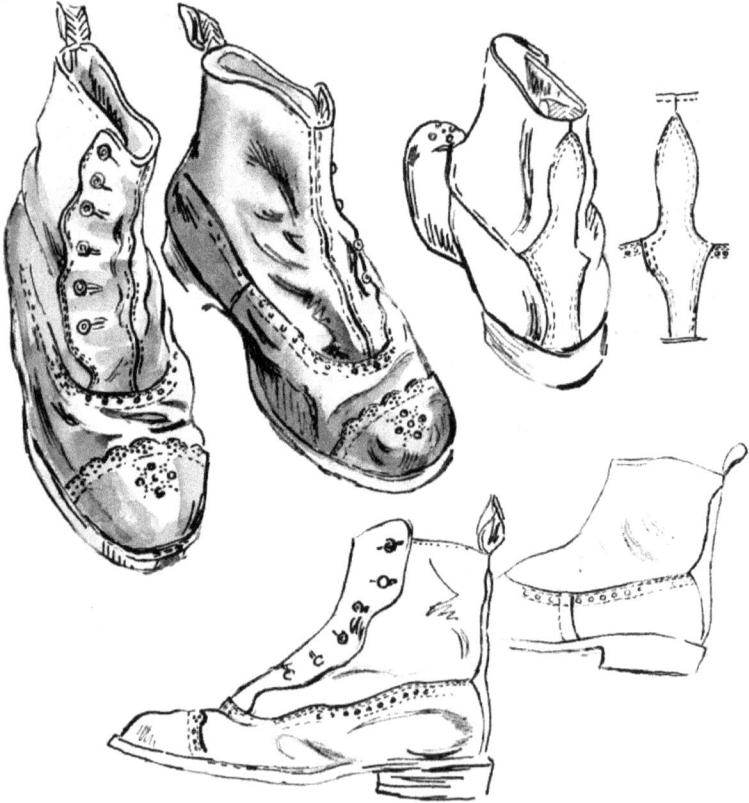

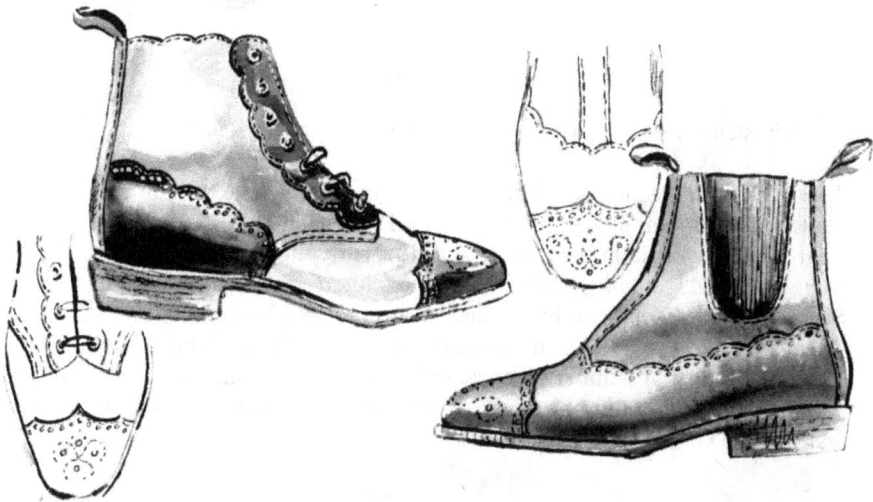

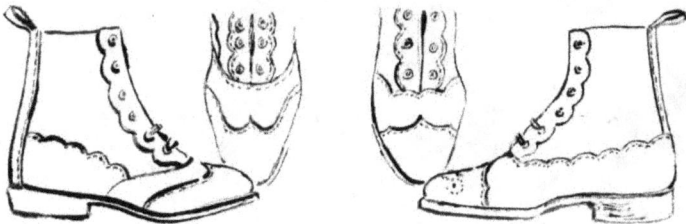

Winstanley of Back Lane, Dublin. Above is one of their boots.

Top right is an elastic-sided boot and a Derby (open fronted) boot and beneath a Balmoral closed front boot – all by Quant and Son. Bottom right is a boot made in the late seventies or early eighties carrying the name Wearside although actually manufactured by the firm Alfred Sargent of Rushden, Northamptonshire, which has been in business since 1899. These boots, which became known as Dealers' boots, are still produced by a number of companies, and some are manufactured abroad. At one time the majority of Gypsy men wore these boots. Now many of the youth prefer the comfort of trainers.

Circa 2007

# CHILDREN'S DRESS

1913

1983

# SUITS

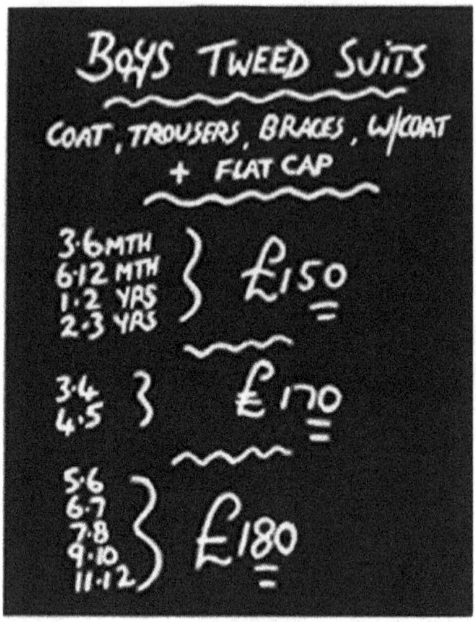

**BOYS TWEED SUITS**

COAT, TROUSERS, BRACES, W/COAT
+ FLAT CAP

3·6 MTH
6·12 MTH
1·2 YRS
2·3 YRS
} £150

3·4
4·5
} £170

5·6
6·7
7·8
9·10
11·12
} £180

**TWEED SHORT SUITS**

6·12  1·2  2·3
3·4  4·5
5·6

£70

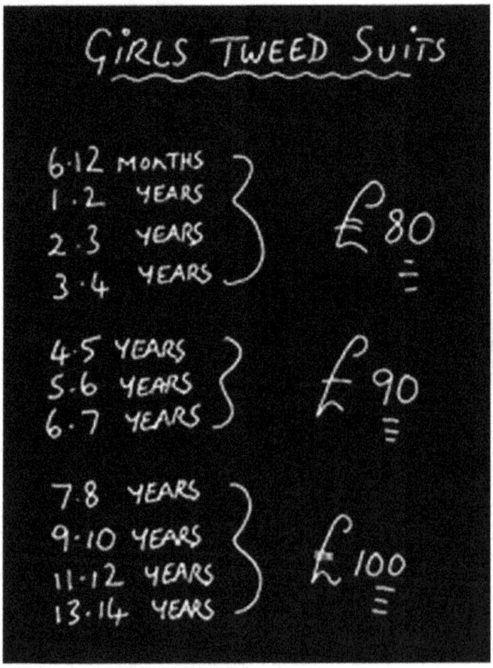

**GIRLS TWEED SUITS**

6·12 MONTHS
1·2 YEARS
2·3 YEARS
3·4 YEARS
} £80

4·5 YEARS
5·6 YEARS
6·7 YEARS
} £90

7·8 YEARS
9·10 YEARS
11·12 YEARS
13·14 YEARS
} £100

TWEED
SHORT SUITS
6-12  12  2-3
3-4  4-5
5-6
£70

GIRLS TWEED SUITS
6-12 months
1-2 years     } £80
2-3 years
3-4 years
4-5 years
5-6 years     } £90
6-7 years
7-8 years
9-10 years    } £100
11-12 years

circa 2007

158

GIRLS TWEED SUITS

| | |
|---|---|
| 6-12 MONTHS | |
| 1-2 YEARS | |
| 2-3 YEARS | £80 |
| 3-4 YEARS | |
| 4-5 YEARS | |
| 5-6 YEARS | £90 |
| 6-7 YEARS | |
| 7-8 YEARS | |
| 9-10 YEARS | |
| 11-12 YEARS | £100 |
| 13-14 YEARS | |

SLIP + CAP

| | |
|---|---|
| 6-12 | |
| 1-2 | |
| 2-3 | £60 |
| 3-4 | |
| 4-5 | |
| 5-6 | £70 |
| 6-7 | |

B+B SET

| | |
|---|---|
| 3-6 | |
| 6-12 | |
| 1-2 | £60 |
| 2-3 | |

2010

# BELTS AND BRACES

Belts and Braces are an important feature of the Gypsy men's dress, for both decorative and practical reasons. The practical side is obvious, based on the lives they lead, and these accessories offer considerable scope for embellishing their dress. The braces, which are sometimes printed with horses heads and horse-shoes, add a splash of colour, while the belts with their large buckles – often horse shoe – add a sparkle to the general ensemble.

Unless Gypsies take to only wearing track-suits, braces and belts will remain important.

In 1979 on a Surrey common, a friend encountered a jogger wearing a blue track-suit. He was astonished to discover that the youth was the son of one of the most old fashioned Gypsy women in the county. This occurrence highlights the folly of trying to stereotype Gypsies.

In the first decade of this century flashy, fancy belts, studded and with large buckles, appeared on the female gaujo market. These exactly matched the Gypsy girls' taste and are still worn to great advantage.

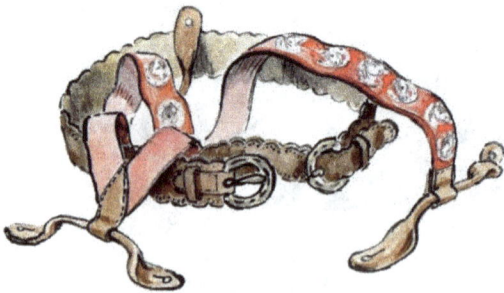

# AFTERWORD

One of the most significant moments of my life was when I first saw Rhona and Will Taylor's turn-out on the side of the Chichester by-pass. They became my first Gypsy friends and over the following half century I made others. Sadly, many have now passed on, but not their memory, and the memory of their faces are contained in this book. Rhona and Will, as well as Sarah West (née Lee), her family and friends made this possible by lending photographs and allowing me to photograph or sketch them, so that I could add authenticity to the illustrations with their portraits. This book is not just about clothes, it is about those who wore them, to whom I owe my first thanks.

There are so many more who have helped me: my husband John, brother Anthony and friend Brian Raywid. Messers Clegg and Perkin of the Sydney Jones Library, University of Liverpool; Antony Hippisley Coxe; Francois de Vaux de Foletier; Andy Holmes; Mervyn Jones; Edward Prior; David Smith; Terry Watson; H. Vandormael; Kasteel van Gaasbeek; Dietmar Winkler, circus and artists' archivist, Berlin; and the many names and credits within the text. All these people have contributed to the realization of this book. My gratitude, above all to the Gypsies, knows no bounds.

# GALLERY

Leather & fur  1985 - 1989

1986 - 1989

1986 - 1989

1989 - 1991

1991 - 1993

172

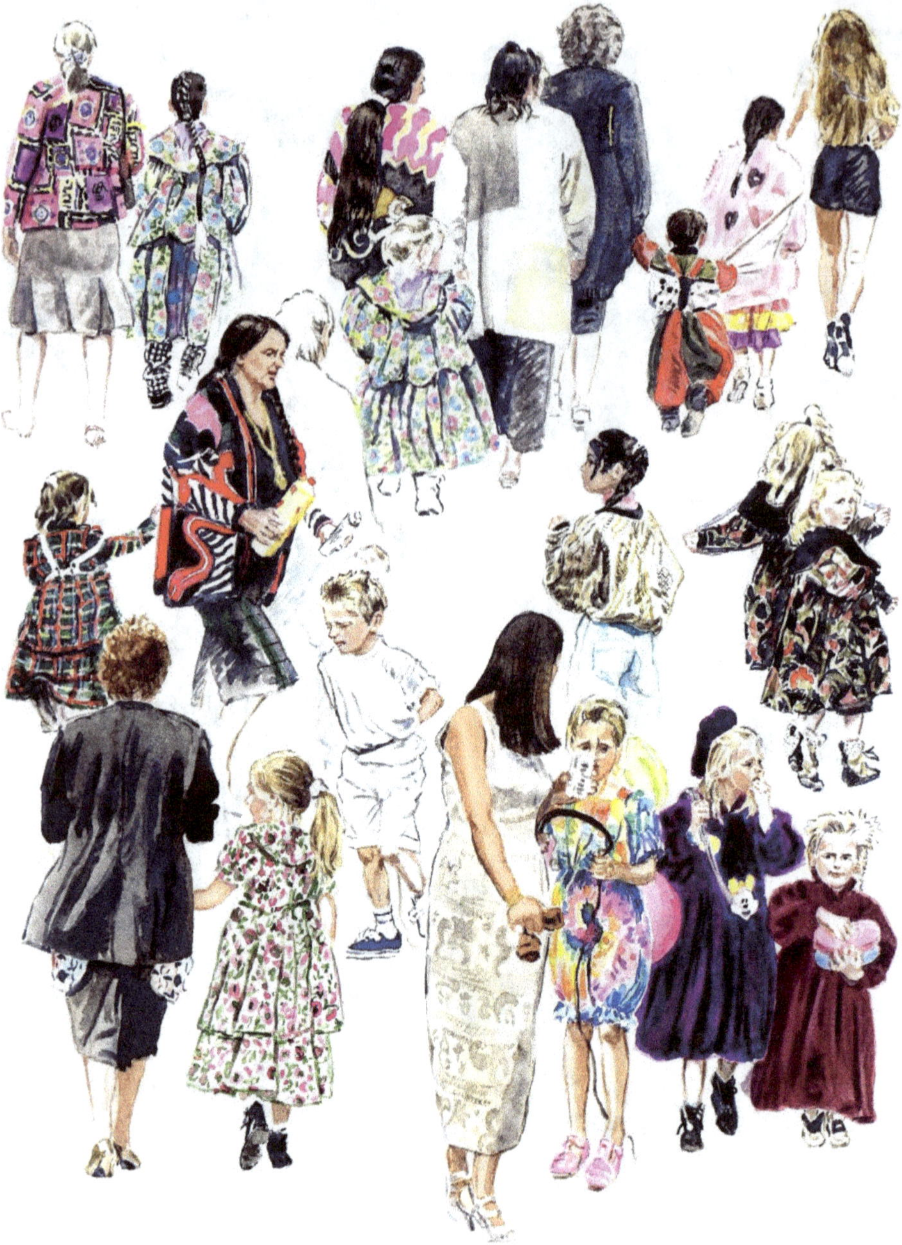

1994 - 1995

Leather, sheepskin & denim  1991 - 1997

1996 - 1997

1998 - 2000

2002 – 2003

2005

2006

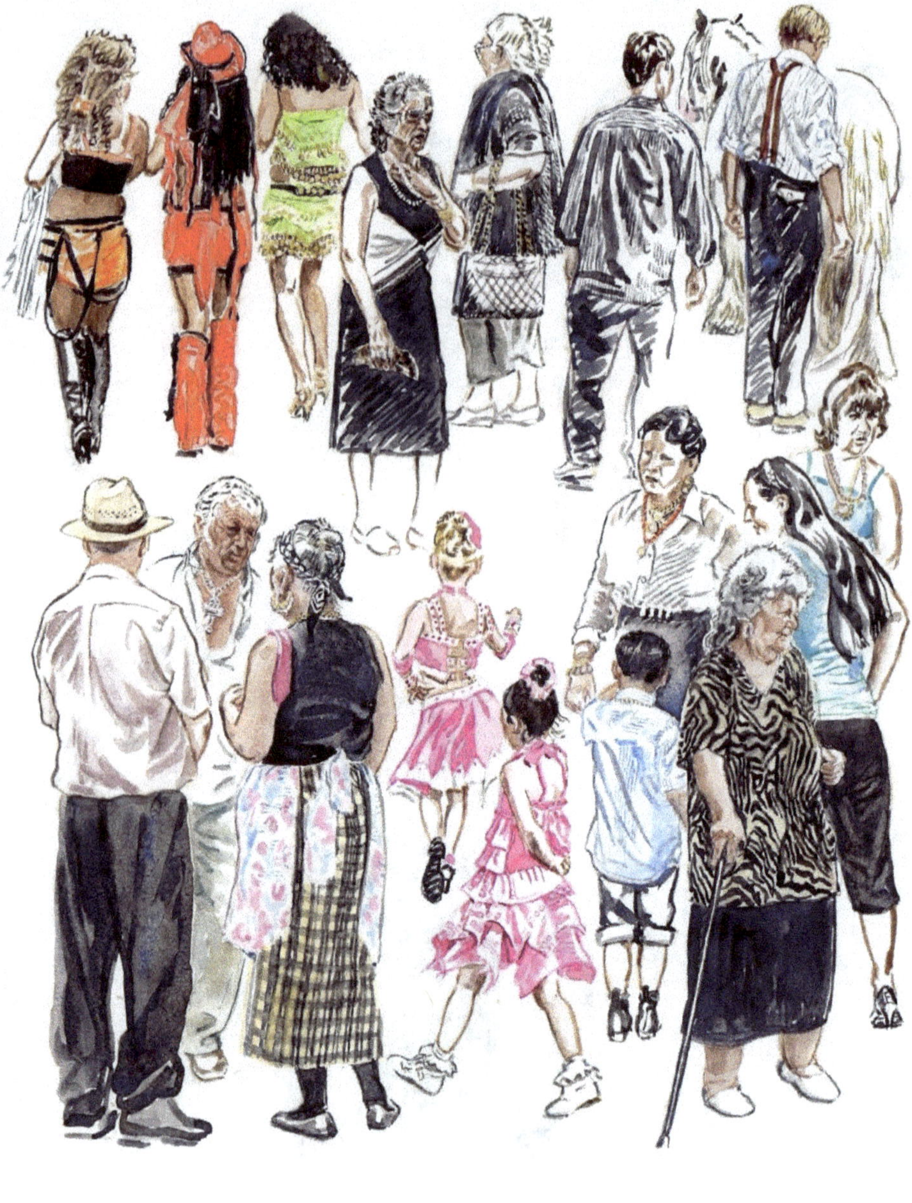

2007

2008

2008

2009

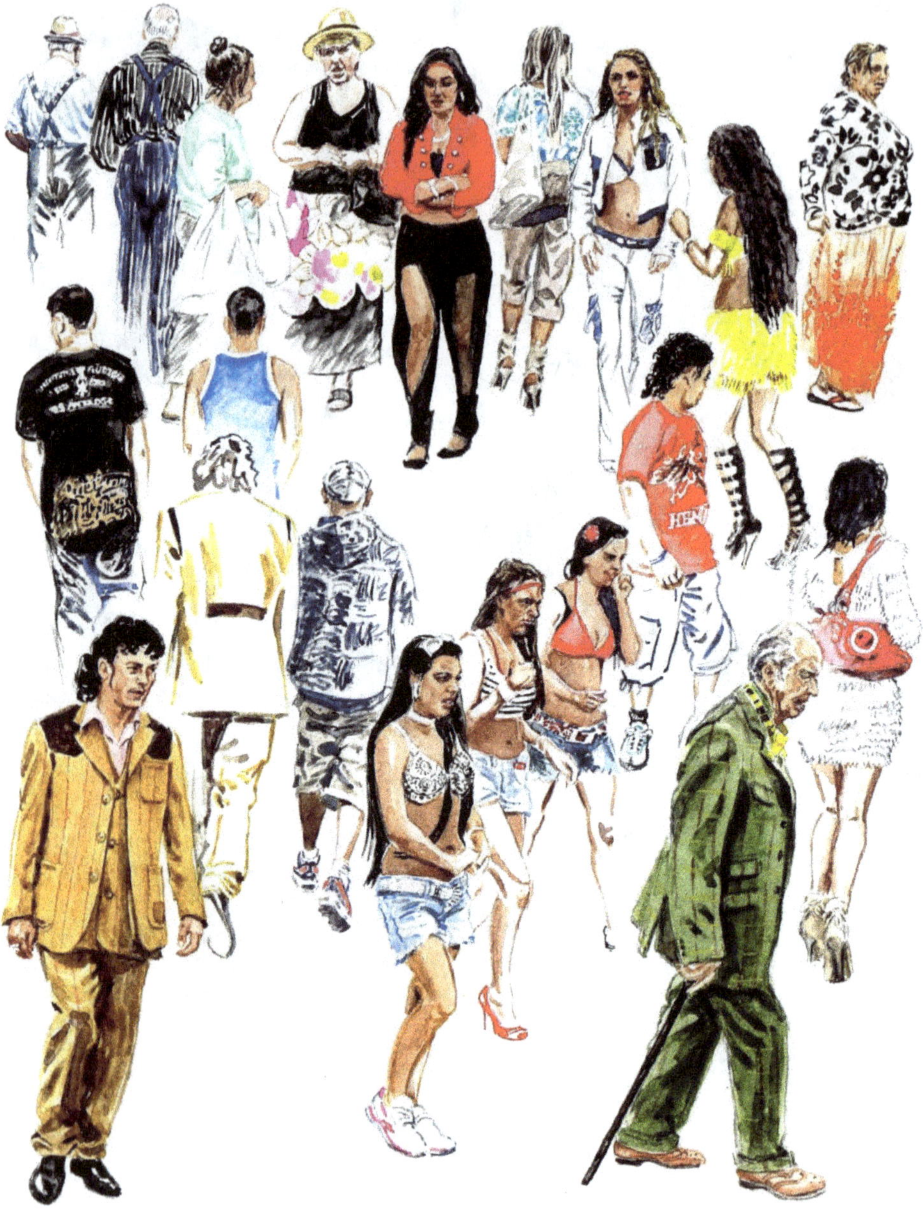

2010

197

2010

# BIBLIOGRAPHY

## GYPSY BOOKS

ARNOLD H. 'Die Zigeuner' Olten et Fribourg-en-Brisgau, Walter 1965
BLOCH J.     'Les Tsiganes' 1953
BLOCK M. 'Gypsies, their Life and their Customs' translated from French
                              1936, Appleton-Century Co. 1939
BORROW George 'The Romany Rye' Murray 1842
BOSWELL Gordon Silvester 'The Book of Boswell' Gollancz 1970
CLEBERT Jean-Paul 'The Gypsies' translated from French by C. Duff
                              Vista 1963, Penguin 1967
COLOCCI Adriano Amerigo 'Gli Zingari' Turin 1883
CROFT-COOKE Rupert 'The Moon in my Pocket' Sampson Low Marston
                              & Co. Ltd. 1948
CUTTRISS Frank 'Romany Life' Mills and Boon 1915
VESEY-FITZGERALD Brian 'Gypsies of Britain' Chapman & Hall 1944,
                              David & Charles 1973 with extra chapter
de VAUX de FOLETIER François 'Le Monde des Tsiganes'
         Berger-Levrault 1983 'Les Tsiganes dans l'ancienne France' Paris
                              Société d'édition géographique & touristique 1961
              'Iconographie des Egyptiens, Précisions sur le costume ancien des
                              Tsiganes' dans Gazette des Beaux-Arts 1966
                    'Mille Ans d'Histoire des Tsiganes' Paris, Fayard 1970
GRELLMANN H. M. G. 'Dissertation on the Gypsies' 1st published
                    Germany 1783 Translated Matthew Raper, P. Elmsley 1787
GROOME F. H. 'In Gypsy Tents' Edin. Nimmo 1880 and E. P. Pub.
                              Wakefield 1973
HALL The Rev. George 'The Gypsy's Parson' Sampson Low Marston &
                              Co. Ltd. 1915
HARVEY Denis 'The Gypsies, Waggon-time and After' Batsford 1979
LYSTER M. Eileen 'The Gypsy Life of Betsy Wood'   J. M. Dent & Sons
                              Ltd. 1926
McEVOY Patrick A. 'The Gorse and the Briar' George G. Harrap 1938
REEVE Dominic 'Smoke in the Lanes' Constable 1958
SAMPSON John 'The Wind on the Heath' A Gypsy Anthology Chatto &
                              Windus 1930
SAMPSON John 'English Gypsy Dress' J.G.L.S. Old Series 1891-2
SIMSON Walter 'A History of the Gypsies' edited by James Simson
         Sampson Low, Marston & Co. Ltd 1865 written at least 20 years earlier
YATES Dora 'My Gypsy Days' Phoenix House Ltd. 1953
J.G.L.S. Journals of the Gypsy Lore Society:
MacRitchie David 'Callot's Bohemiens'&'Gypsy Colours' Old S.1890

Lovarini E. 'Costumes – Italian Zingaresche' Old Series 1891-2
Yoxall J. H. 'A Word on Gypsy Costume' New Series 1907-8
Crofton Henry T. 'The former Costume of the Gypsies' 1909  Writer un-
                                    known 'The Gypsy Blanket 1910
Winstedt E. O. 'Romany Costume - 19th Century' 1910-11
                         'Gypsy Coppersmiths Invasion of 1911-13' 1913
                                    See also Miss Pardoe's Hungarian Gypsies
Hall Rev. G. 'Turning Garments Inside Out' New Series 1912-13
Thompson T. W. 'English Gypsy Death & Burial Customs'    Third Series
                    Vol III Parts 1 & 2 1924 & Vol IX Part 1 1930
Bartlett D. M. M. 'Two Recent Gypsy Funerals' Third Series 1934
Haley William J. 'Artists Gypsies' 1936
Myers John 'Lazzy Smith in Egglestone's Notebook' 1937
Hammill Alfred E. 'A Fifteenth Century Tapestry' Third Series 1949
Hammill Alfred E. 'David Teniers and the Fortune Teller' 1950
Payne Ffransis G. 'Two Gypsy Scenes in Tapestries' 1950
McFarlane Andrew 'George Morland as an Illustrator of English Gypsy
                                    Life' 1954
Blair F. G. 'The Costume of Gypsies in the Masque' 1954
Partington Ruth 'The Gypsy and the Holy Family' Rest on the flight into
                                    Egypt painted by Paris Bordonne 1956
Starkie Walter 'Jerome Bosch's The Haywain' 1957
Huth Fred 'English Gypsy Dress in Bygone Days: Parts 1 & 2 1959/60
Yates Dora E. 'Bruegel's Sermon of St. John the Baptist' 1965


# GENERAL BOOKS

BAINES John, Jaromir Malek 'Atlas of Ancient Egypt' Phaidon 1958
BORCHARD George  Polish article in the Journal of the Costume Society
                                    no. 4 1970
BOUCHER Francois 'A History of Costume in the West'  Thames &
                                    Hudson 1967
BRADFIELD Nancy 'Historical Costumes of England'  George G. Harrap
                                    1958
BRUHN W.& TILKE M. 'Pictorial History of Costume' Zwemmer 1955
BUCK Anne & CUNNINGTON Phillis 'Children's Costume in England
                    1300-1900' A & C Black Ltd. 1965
CHANDRA Moti 'Costumes, Textiles etc. in Ancient and Mediaeval India'
                                    Delhi 1973
CUNNINGTON P. & LUCAS C. 'Costume for Births, Marriages &
                                    Deaths' A & C Black 1972

CUNNINGTON P. & WILLETT C. 'Handbook of English Costume in the
19th Century' Faber & Faber 1970
CUNNINGTON P. 'Costume in Pictures' Herbert Press 1964

DAR S. N. 'Costumes of India & Pakistan, a Historical & Cultural Study'
D. B. Taraporeval Sons Co. Bombay 1969
DAVENPORT N. 'The Book of Costume' Crown, NY 1948
FORBIS William H. 'Fall of the Peacock Throne: the Story of Iran'
Harper & Row Ltd. 1980
GHURYE G. S. 'Indian Costume' Bombay 1951
GILBEY Sir Walter 'Hounds in Old Days' ed. C. M. F. Scott first pub.
1913) Spur Publications 1979
GILBEY Sir Walter & CUMING E. D. 'George Morland his Life & Work'
A & C Black 1907
GOBEL H. 'Wandteppiche' Leipzig 1923
HACKWOOD Frederick W. 'The Good old Times: the romance of humble
life in England' Unwin, London 1910
HANSEN Henny Harald 'Costume Cavalcade' Methuen 1956
HARRIS J. R. 'The Legacy of Egypt' Oxford 1971
HEINZ D. 'Europainsche Wandtappiche'
HILER H. 'From Nudity to Raiment, an Introduction to the study of
Costume' Foyle 1929
HOUSTON Mary G. 'Ancient Greek, Roman & Byzantine Costume &
Décoration' A & C Black 1931
HOWITT William 'Rural Life of England' Longman, Brown, Green &
Longmans 1838
JOBE Joseph 'The Art of Tapestry' Thames & Hudson 1965
KNIGHT'S 'Old England' Charles Knight & Co. London 1845
KOHLER Carl 'History of Costume' Dover 1963
LACROIX 'Moeurs, usages et costumes au Moyen Age' Paris 1871
LAVER James 'Costume through the Ages' Thames & Hudson 1964
MARILLER H. C. 'Handbook to the Teniers Tapestries Oxford 1932
MAYER J. A. 'Mamluk Costume: a Survey' A Kundig, Geneva 1952
WILLIAMS-MITCHELL Christobel 'Dressed for the Job' Blandford 1982
OAKES Alma & HAMILTON HILL M. 'Rural Costume its Origin &
Development in Western Europe & the British Isles' Batsford 1970
PUCKLE Bertram S. 'Funeral Customs Their Origin & Development'
T. Werner Laurie Ltd. London 1926
RENSON G. & CASTEELS M. 'Prospections dans les collections du
chateau - musee de Gaasbeek' Le Folklore Brabancon no.170 1966
'Het-Kasteel - musee van Gaasbeek' Lennik (Gaasbeek) 1979
RUBENS Alfred 'A History of Jewish Costume' Peter Owen 1967

SHARP Cecil J. & MACLLWAINE H. C. 'The Morris Book'   Novello,
London 1907

SICHEL Marion 'Costume of the Classical World' Batsford 1980

SNOWDEN James 'The Folk Dress of Europe' Mills & Boon 1977

SWANN June 'Shoes' Batsford 1982

STUBBS George 1724-1806 Tate Gallery 1984

TAYLOR Lou 'Mourning Dress: a Costume & Social History' George
Allen & Unwin 1983

VECELLIO Cesare 'Habiti Antichi, et Moderni di Tutto il Mondo' Gio-
vanni Bernardo Sessa, Venice 1590 & 1598 'Vecellio's Renaissance
Costume Book' Dover 1977

WEST R. 'Tapestries of the Lowlands' 1974

TURNER WILCOX R. 'The Dictionary of Costume'   Scribner, NewYork
1969, B. T. Batsford 1970 & 1973

WILSON Lillian 'The Roman Toga' John Hopkins 1924

YARWOOD Doreen 'English Costume from the 2nd Century BC to the
Present Day' Batsford 1952

'European Costume 4000 Years of Fashion' Batsford 1975

'Encyclopaedia of World Costume' Batsford 1978

OTHER BOOKS WRITTEN AND ILLUSTRATED BY JULIET JEFFERY

Gypsy Vans    Author published    1983

A Tiny Tale    Author published    1998

Sarah's Tales – Celebrating the Life of Sarah West – in two volumes Author published    2010

Gypsy Guise and Disguise – LIMITED EDITION*    Author published 2018    (see below)


BOOKS ILLUSTRATED BY JULIET JEFFERY

The Gypsy – Poems and Ballads by Lavengro        Midas Books 1973

Bender Tents by Edward Ayres    Macmillan Education    1979

Appleby Fair by Barbara Applin    Macmillan Press    1980

*This book is also available in a cloth-bound limited edition (25.6x18cm), colour printed on Heritage Book-white paper, sewn binding with excellent open flat quality: £95 plus p&p direct from the author who can be contacted via Lamorna publications.

www.ingramcontent.com/pod-product-compliance
Lightning Source LLC
Chambersburg PA
CBHW061731270326
41928CB00011B/2186